REMEMBER THE DAYS

The aim of Zenith Books is to present the history of minority groups in the United States and their participation in the growth and development of the country. Through histories and biographies written by leading historians in collaboration with established writers for young people, Zenith Books will increase awareness of and at the same time develop an understanding and appreciation for minority group heritage.

Dr. John Hope Franklin, Chairman of the History Department at the University of Chicago, has also taught at Brooklyn College, Fisk University, and Howard University. For the year 1962–63, he was William Pitt Professor of American History and Institutions at Cambridge University in England. He is the author of many books, including *From Slavery to Freedom, The Militant South, Reconstruction After the Civil War,* and *The Emancipation Proclamation.* In April 1974 Dr. Franklin was elected President of the Organization of American Historians.

Milton Meltzer is both a historian and a biographer, and is the author of more than twenty-five books. He has written biographies of Thoreau, Twain, Margaret Sanger, Thaddeus Stevens, and many others. Among his recent works are *Slavery,* a two-volume world history; *World of Our Fathers: The Jews of Eastern Europe;* and *The Eye of Conscience: Photographers and Social Change.* Mr. Meltzer collaborated with Langston Hughes on *A Pictorial History of Blackamericans.* His biography of Mr. Hughes was nominated for the National Book Award.

Melvin I. Urofsky, consultant on this book, teaches history in the Allen Center at the State University of New York at Albany. He received his doctorate from Columbia University and has taught at Ohio State University. He is the co-editor of *The Brandeis Letters* and the author of *Big Steel and the Wilson Administration, Why Teachers Strike,* and *Perspectives on Urban America.*

Harvey Dinnerstein was born in New York City in 1928. He grew up in the Brownsville section of Brooklyn, a neighborhood then consisting mostly of Jewish immigrants struggling to survive in the midst of the Depression. Many of the illustrations in this book derive from family recollections of the old country and immigrant life in America. Mr. Dinnerstein was educated at the High School of Music and Art in New York City, and the Tyler School of Art of Temple University in Philadelphia. He was awarded the Temple Gold Medal of the Pennsylvania Academy, and has received two Tiffany Foundation Grants.

REMEMBER THE DAYS

A Short History of the Jewish American

MILTON MELTZER
Illustrated by Harvey Dinnerstein

ZENITH BOOKS
Doubleday & Company, Inc., Garden City, New York, 1974

The Zenith Books edition, published simultaneously in hardbound and paper-
back volumes, is the first publication of REMEMBER THE DAYS.
Zenith Books Edition: 1974

Doubleday gratefully acknowledges the resources of the *Yivo Institute for Jewish Research* for their assistance in researching the paintings for this book.

Library of Congress Cataloging in Publication Data
Meltzer, Milton, 1915–
  Remember the days.

  SUMMARY: A short history of the Jews in America
from 1654 and their first permanent community of
twenty-three persons in New Amsterdam to the present,
stressing the difficulties they have continually faced
as an ethnic minority.
  1. Jews in the United States—History—Juvenile
literature. [1. Jews in the United States—History]
I. Dinnerstein, Harvey, illus. II. Title.
E184.J5M45 1974   917.3′06′924
ISBN 0-385-05946-9 Trade
      0-385-07676-2 Paperbound
Library of Congress Catalog Card Number 74–5532

For Solomon Balinky

CONTENTS

Remember the days of old,
consider the years of many generations;
ask thy father and he will shew thee,
thy elders and they will tell thee.

Deuteronomy 32:7
Old Testament

REMEMBER THE DAYS

Chapter 1

THE MIGRATION BEGINS

"I was born into a self-contained Yiddish ghetto," wrote Harry Roskolenko. "It was the lowest part of the East Side amid crowded-together, five-story, wash-hung tenements. Everything was immigrant-laden, a bazaar of colors and bizarre language. Though we were the majority, the ghetto also had Poles, Russians, Irish, and Italians. All of us had our special places, dictated to us by our faces, our speech, our jobs, our music, dances, and books—and, of course, our religion and country of origin. Each lived in a ghetto within a ghetto. Did we mind it? We wanted to be among our own people, our own language, our own religion, and to be ourselves down to our last Jewish roots."

That was New York in the year 1907. Then, the word "ghetto" in most people's minds still meant a place where Jewish people lived. The word probably came from the Italian *gietto*, the cannon foundry at Venice near which the first Jewish settlement in the city was located about a thousand years ago. In time that ghetto became not simply the quarter where Jews lived, but the place where they were *forced* to live—where they were walled away from other people.

Nowadays the term "ghetto" is no longer limited to the Jews. It applies to any segregated ethnic or cultural group. For the Jews, the history of the ghetto has been in large part the history of their people since the Romans conquered Palestine and destroyed Jerusalem. Then—in 70 C.E.—began the long period of migration in search of new homes. ("Diaspora," or "dispersion," is the word for it.)

The Jews go back in time to the patriarch Abraham, whose people were among the nomadic tribes of Palestine wandering the desert four thousand years ago. Calling themselves Israelites, they settled on the coastal plains of Canaan. Upon the founding of the Kingdom of Judah, they became known as Jews.

The Roman conquest of their state dispersed the Jews to the far corners of the earth. Many joined Jewish communities established much earlier, in Babylonia, Egypt, Syria, Rome, the Aegean islands. Others founded new communities in Poland, the Rhineland, Italy, Spain, France, England.

But though torn away from their capital city and their Temple, the Jews kept their faith. To affirm it they need only live by the Commandments and carry out good works. Each local community learned to rely upon itself to maintain the sacred teachings and the laws of Judaism. Gradually the synagogue, with its simple service of prayers and hymns, became the center of religious life.

Believing that ignorance led to sin, the Jews placed study high as one of the ways to the kingdom of Heaven. The synagogues were as much schools as houses of prayer. And devotion to knowledge became a special quality of Judaism.

Throughout the medieval centuries the Jews were only a tolerated group. From the early 300s, when the Christian Church became the state religion under Constantine, it insisted Christianity was the true religion, the only religion. The Jews resisted conversion. They could not give up Judaism lightly. The Church used state power to make the Jews outcasts, with no citizenship or rights. The Jews were set apart and treated much the way South Africa treats blacks today. The anti-Jewish laws became woven into the way people thought, a pattern that still exists to this day.

Stripped of rights, the Jews could do nothing without permission of emperor, king, lord, or bishop. The honorable ways to make a living were denied them. They could not hold land or practice agriculture. Though engaged in many crafts before this time, now the guilds excluded them. Trade was the only choice left. Christians were not supposed to enter trade, so the Jews became merchants wandering about with peddlers' packs.

Judaism neither encouraged nor opposed trade. It accepted it as necessary, and tried to regulate it as it did all aspects of Jewish life. Later, as economies developed and trade became attractive to Christians, the Jews were displaced. They had to turn to banking and finance. Here too, as a country became more advanced, Jewish financiers were replaced by Christians.

It was these centuries that saw the rise of the legend of the Jew as capitalist and usurer, with the hateful "Shylock" label pinned to him. The merchants too, like the craftsmen, eventually shut their guilds to the Jews. No wonder most Jews in medieval times were poor, and stayed poor. They lived an uncertain existence. To survive amid strangers and enemies they had to move about a great deal and adapt to constantly changing conditions. "Their settlements, such as they were," wrote one scholar, were "mere stopping places on a road that led they knew not where."

As transients in western Europe, they played a great role in the exchange not only of commercial products but of ideas. The expansion and deepening of culture in the early medieval world owed much to Jewish learning. Jewish physicians, philosophers, translators, financiers, serving princes of state and Church, helped waken Europe to a fresh intellectual life.

When the Crusades began in 1095, the militant Church turned to a policy of active oppression which led in many places to wholesale slaughter and expulsion. Why go to redeem the Holy Land, preachers asked, if we leave untouched the Jewish enemy in our midst? There was a greedy motive too behind these massacres. Kill a Jewish merchant or moneylender and you could seize his goods or cancel the debt you owed him.

Having no right to protect themselves, the Jews were forced

to buy protection from princes and popes. Some won—at a price —a degree of security from rulers who looked upon them as mere sources of income. An emperor kept Jews as his right, and often sold that right to other people much as he would any other commodity. The Jew was less a man than simply taxable property. He had to place his hope for survival not in the law, but in the ruler's personal whim.

In 1215 the Church's Fourth Lateran Council ordered Jews to wear a yellow patch on their clothing. The distinctive badge humiliated the Jew and made him an easy target for mobs that saw him as the "murderer of Christ." The Council decreed too that Jews must live apart from Christians. So the Jews were driven relentlessly within the confining walls of the ghetto. They were forced to live in narrow, dark streets, in crowded, crumbling houses, behind barred and bolted gates. From dusk to daybreak no Jew could leave the ghetto. If found outside the walls, he was heavily punished.

Anti-Jewish feeling spread like an infection. The Church failed to cure popular ignorance, fear, and superstition. Everything that went wrong in life was assumed to be the work of an evildoer. The Jews were plainly the guilty ones. They had to be driven out or killed. When the Black Death devastated Europe in the 1340s, the Jews were accused of poisoning the water supplies. Many Jewish communities were massacred. Their synagogues were burned over their heads; they died singing Psalms.

"Measured in terms of duration, magnitude, and conscious suffering," wrote the historian Friedrich Heer, "there is nothing in the history of Europe, or even of the world, to compare with the martyrdom of the Jews of medieval Europe. Non-Jewish and Christian historians should feel it their solemn duty to put the facts on record."

It was this persecution that started another great wave of migration. Jews in Germany and central Europe fled to Poland and the eastern regions. Jews in southern Spain moved up the peninsula to Castile. Jews of Provence migrated into France and Italy. From England, Jews fled to the continent. Constant oppression meant constant migration. The injustice, the suffering, went on and on, leaving its mark on Jewish thought.

The King and Queen of Spain expelled the Jews in 1492. In his diary Christopher Columbus noted the coincidence: "In the same month in which Their Majesties issued the edict that all Jews should be driven out of the kingdom and its territories, in the same month they gave me the order to undertake with sufficient men my expedition of discovery to the Indies."

The Jews had known a Golden Age in Spain for several hundred years. They had arrived in large numbers when the African Moors conquered southern Spain in the eighth century. The enlightened Mohammedans encouraged the Jews to develop their own religious and communal life. Jewish thinkers shared with learned Arabs in the nurture of every branch of the arts and sciences. One of the Jews' most valued services was to translate into Latin many scholarly and scientific works originally written in Greek, Arabic, or Hebrew. But they were not only carriers of this rich material out of which was fashioned much of what we call Western or Christian civilization. They also made many contributions of their own to science and culture.

When the power of the Moors was broken, the position of the Jews crumbled. From 1411 the Inquisition combined the force of Church and state to convert the reluctant Jews. Violence and treachery were used. Many Jews chose baptism rather than death. Most were new Christians only in form, secretly practicing Judaism. They were called marranos. They made careers in government, army, and university, in finance and trade, even in the Church. In 1478, under the Grand Inquisitor, Torquemada, Spain began a reign of terror against the Jews. Thousands were tortured, condemned to rot in dungeons, or burned at the stake. Finally, at Torquemada's request, Ferdinand and Isabella ordered the Jews out of Spain. They were allowed to take out nothing. They scattered in all directions: south to Africa, north to Portugal, east to Greece and Turkey.

Many chose to stay in Spain at the heavy price of baptism. Some were sold into slavery, some escaped into death.

The Golden Age of Jewish civilization in Spain had ended in horror. But west, across the uncharted Atlantic Ocean, a new age was about to begin.

Chapter 2

BECOMING AMERICAN

It is a curious footnote to Spain's history to record the role of the Jews in making that country's expeditions to the New World a success. A Jew prepared the charts Columbus relied on, a Jew compiled his almanacs and astronomical tables, Jews gave him financial backing. The physician on his flagship was a Jew, and so was the ship's surgeon. The first man he put ashore in the Americas, his official interpreter, was said to have been a Jew. There are several historians who think Columbus himself was secretly a Jew.

But Jews expelled from the mother country were not likely to seek homes in its New World colonies. Not until the terror of the Spanish Inquisition had lessened somewhat did Jews settle in the West Indies and Latin America. Most had stopped for refuge in Holland or elsewhere before sailing across the Atlantic. Brazil became the haven for many while the Dutch controlled it. Then the Portuguese ousted the Dutch, and the Jews in Brazil again faced death or expulsion.

Out of these troubles came the first permanent community of Jews in what is now the United States. It was September 1, 1654, when the *Saint Charles* sailed into New York harbor, then New Amsterdam. Aboard were twenty-three Jewish passengers fleeing from the Portuguese in Brazil. Like the Pilgrims who had landed at Plymouth Rock thirty-four years earlier, they were seeking freedom from persecution. In the stormy voyage the Jews had lost most of their belongings. Whatever was left they had to auction off to pay the ship's captain. The governor of New Amsterdam, Peter Stuyvesant, wrote the Dutch East India Company in Holland for permission to kick out the penniless refugees. He gave the usual anti-Semitic reasons: the Jews were usurers, deceitful, burdensome. And, he added, he did not want "to infect" New Amsterdam with "such hateful enemies . . . of Christ." (The governor had already shown his bigotry by persecuting Lutherans and Quakers in the colony.)

The Jews of old Amsterdam in Holland, who had a financial interest in the West India Company, argued to let the new colonists stay. Would they not face greater danger if deported to Spain or Portugal? Had they not risked their property and their blood to defend Dutch interests in Brazil? Didn't the French and the English permit Jews in their colonies?

Stuyvesant was ordered to admit the Jews. But he did not mean to make life easy for them. He barred them from owning land, trading with the Indians, entering any craft, holding public office, or practicing their religion in a synagogue or public gathering. He would not let them share guard duty while in place of it he ordered them to pay a tax.

The Jews refused to accept such discrimination. One of the refugees, young Asser Levy, a butcher by trade, declared he was fit to keep guard, and would not pay the tax. He won his point, and the Jews were allowed to defend the colony. Under Levy's leadership the Jews fought every step up the ladder to full citizenship. In 1664, New Amsterdam was captured by the English and renamed New York. But because treatment of the Jews in England lagged behind the standard won in Holland, the Jews of New York had to renew the struggle for equal rights. The New World could not escape the conflicts of the Old.

No harm came to the colony because the Jews were allowed to stay. It proved how untrue Stuyvesant's case against them was. What had he hoped to gain by his anti-Semitism? Probably

Under the Grand Inquisitor, Spain began a reign of terror against the Jews. They were tortured, condemned to dungeons, or burned at the stake.

to keep himself in power by putting down the Jews and other minorities.

The Puritans who settled in New England loved the biblical Hebrews and taught their ancient language in the colleges. But they did not welcome their descendants, the Jews. They would not open their towns to the Jews as a community, but only to individuals they hoped to convert.

The next Jewish settlement was established in Newport, Rhode Island, in 1658. It was the sole New England colony to invite the oppressed of all sects. Rhode Island's founder, Roger Williams, was among the first Americans to champion freedom of conscience and the rights of Jews and Indians. "I humbly conceive it to be the duty of the civil magistrate," he wrote, "to break down that superstitious wall of separation (as to civil things) between the Gentiles and the Jews, and freely without their asking to make way for their peaceable habitation among us."

There is mention of individual Jews in the New England colonies during the seventeenth century. Not until the eighteenth, however, did Jewish communities gain footholds elsewhere. The Carolina Constitution assured religious toleration to "Jews, heathens and other dissenters" and enough Jews were in Charleston by 1750 to found a congregation. Georgia's first governor, James Oglethorpe, overcame bigoted opposition to permit two boatloads of Jews to settle there. Under William Penn's policy of religious liberty for all, Jews were able to organize a community at Philadelphia about 1745. From there some went west to settle the colony's frontier.

On the eve of the American Revolution it is estimated there were only 1000 to 2500 Jews in the colonies. Many came in search of the better livelihood the colonies promised; some came fleeing religious persecution; others came as indentured servants. They made up less than one tenth of 1 per cent of the total population of some three million. Most of the Jews were of Spanish and Portuguese descent. They were called Sephardim. But a good many others were of Ashkenazi origin—that is, from Germany, England, France, or eastern Europe. The

Jews lived chiefly in seaboard towns—Newport, New York, Philadelphia, Charleston, Savannah. They were used to city life. Unlike most newcomers to America they were not farmers. Their ancestors had worked in European cities for generations. They had to stay in cities if they were to keep up a community and maintain a synagogue.

Some did give up their Jewish life. They intermarried with neighbors, and most of their descendants disappeared into the general community. Those who remained faithful built a community life around their synagogues. The synagogue became the center for education, philanthropy, and social activities as well as for worship.

Few though the Jews were, they played a useful part in commercial and social life. They lived side by side with the Gentiles. There were no ghettos, and no bars to Jews owning property. Jewish merchants were busy in trade between the colonies and abroad, as well as with the Indians. Some helped open up the West, dealing in lands and trading in furs. Some became artisans and craftsmen. Jews in Newport developed the sperm-oil industry, in Georgia introduced viniculture (the cultivation of grapes), and in South Carolina became the leading indigo growers. Partnerships were not uncommon between Jews and non-Jews.

The best-known Jew in the colonies was Newport's Aaron Lopez, a Portuguese immigrant. By 1775, with a stake in more than thirty ships, he was a key figure in the trade with the West Indies, Europe, and Africa.

When the Revolution broke out, most of the Jews served the cause of freedom. Since many were merchants and tradesmen, they were among the first to suffer from Britain's restrictive measures. Throughout the struggle for independence, Revolutionary leaders summoned up the biblical people, who had liberated themselves from Egyptian oppression, as an example and inspiration. Some Jews, like many Christians, remained loyalists, putting their mercantile connections with Britain above the interests of the new republic. Only a small number of the Jews were young enough to bear arms. About one hundred fought, many of them earning honor and distinction. A French Jew from Bordeaux, Benjamin Nones, came over to volunteer in the Revolutionary Army, serving under Washington, Pulaski, and Lafayette. Other Jews, like Haym Solomon, helped the cause by raising funds for equipping and provisioning the Army. The whole Shearith Israel congregation, rather than live under British occupation, moved out of New York City. Their minister, Gershom Seixas, preached patriotic sermons from his pulpit. Jews were among the privateers who did important service by raiding British vessels at sea.

The Jewish people did their part in birthing a new nation dedicated to the democratic principle that "all men are created equal."

The constitutions of the individual states fixed no religious qualifications for voting (except in New Hampshire). But apart from Rhode Island, New York, and South Carolina, they specified that only Christians could hold office, in spite of the preambles which proclaimed the natural rights of man.

Political rights were the last to be won, not only for the Jews, but for Catholics, deists, or non-believers. The victory was not gained until 1826 in Maryland and 1868 in North Carolina. The rights enjoyed by the Jews in the courts and their chances for fair trial were better in early America than those of other minority groups. The Catholics, for one, and of course blacks and Indians.

When one minority group won protection of the laws, the others were likely to benefit from it. Security for one promised security for all. Rarely, however, for blacks and Indians.

Pressed by Thomas Jefferson and James Madison, Virginia adopted a Religious Freedom Act in 1785. It paved the way for a similar clause in the Northwest Ordinance of 1787. A few months later, the Founding Fathers wrote into the U. S. Constitution that "no religious test shall ever be required as to qualification for any office or public trust under the United States" (Article VI, Section 3). When the Bill of Rights was added to the Constitution, the First Amendment guaranteed freedom of religion to all, and barred Congress from establishing any Church as the privileged religion of the nation.

No longer did Jews have to feel they were "tolerated." Here they were not outcasts, the despised of the earth. When Newport Jews congratulated George Washington on his election as the first President, he replied in a famous letter which stressed the equality of all Americans, regardless of creed:

> All possess alike liberty of conscience and immunities of citizenship. It is now no more that toleration is spoken of, as if it was by the indulgence of one class of people, that another enjoyed the exercise of their inherent natural rights. For, happily, the government of the United States which gives to bigotry no sanction, to persecution no assistance, requires only that they who live under its protection, should demean themselves as good citizens . . .
>
> May the children of the stock of Abraham who dwell in this land, continue to merit and enjoy the good will of the other inhabitants; while everyone shall sit in safety under his own vine and fig-tree, and there shall be none to make him afraid.

Where discriminatory laws still existed, Jews fought to eliminate them. Campaigns were waged in New Hampshire, North Carolina, and Pennsylvania to secure for Jews the rights all other citizens enjoyed.

There were few such legal barriers for Jews, nor were there any acts of violence against them by government. Underneath, however, there always ran a current of prejudice which surfaced in time of crisis. When Jefferson's progressive Republican movement was battling for power with the conservative Federalists, Jews supporting the Jeffersonians were attacked as Jews. Prejudice was used as a political weapon.

In 1800, a letter appeared in *The Gazette of the United States* slandering Benjamin Nones, the Revolutionary War veteran supporting Jefferson. The writer smeared Jews, Negroes, workers, the poor, and the democratic goals of the Republicans. Nones made a public reply, saying in part:

> I am accused of being a Jew; of being a Republican; and of being Poor.
> I am a Jew. I glory in belonging to that persuasion . . . I am a Jew. I am so—and so were Abraham, and Isaac, and Moses and the prophets, and so too were Christ and his apostles, I feel no disgrace in ranking with such society . . .
> I am a Jew, and if for no other reason, for that reason I am a Republican. Among the pious priesthood of church establishments, we are compassionately ranked with Turks, Infidels and Heretics. In the monarchies of Europe, we are hunted from society—stigmatized as unworthy of common civility, thrust out as it were from the converse of men; objects of mockery and insult to forward children, the butts of vulgar wit, and low buffoonery . . .
> Among the nations of Europe we are inhabitants everywhere—but Citizens nowhere unless in Republics. Here, in France, and in the Batavian Republic alone, we are treated as men and as brethren. In republics we have rights, in monarchies we live but to experience wrongs . . .

By the early 1800s, the pattern of the peopling of America was clear. English, Scots, Scotch-Irish, and Germans composed more than four fifths of the population. The Jews were a handful among them. Like all the others, they came for a mixture of reasons—seeking freedom from persecution, and freedom to make a decent living. Each immigrant, unhappy where he was, hoped it might be better someplace else.

The Anglo-Saxons, by far the largest single group of immigrants, put their lasting stamp upon the new nation. Their language became the language of all, their political and social forms took root and grew here. In the Declaration of Independence they pledged to make one nation out of an America of uprooted peoples. In the Constitution, they made the tragic mistake of compromising with slavery. Still, they gave life to the creed of human rights. Ever since, there has been the struggle to resolve the conflict between the offer of brotherhood and the reality of poverty and prejudice. The Jews who would come in increasing numbers would share with the millions of other immigrants the cost of becoming American.

Chapter 3

THE GERMAN WAVE

Not until 1836 did the first mass migration of Jews to America begin. The flow of all immigration from Europe had been cut off by the Napoleonic Wars. When the fighting ended in 1815, individual Jews and single families trickled in again. But now something new was seen. Whole communities of Jews from a single town or region picked up and set off for the United States. They came from Germany.

For a while, Europe's Jews had been making their way out of the ghetto. Under the banners of the French Revolution, carried across the continent by Napoleon's armies, the Jews had been emancipated. As the ghetto gates came tumbling down, the age of medievalism ended. Foremost among the awakening Jews was Moses Mendelssohn, the son of a poor Torah scribe in Germany. The little hunchback philosopher helped prepare his people to enter the modern world. He knew the ghetto within each Jew had to be destroyed, too, and the ignorance, backwardness, and hopelessness of centuries rooted out. He translated the Bible into German so the Jews might learn the language of the people around them, and provided a new commentary with a rational explanation of Judaism. The movement for enlightenment, called the Haskala, spread to Poland and Russia. Once again the Hebrew of the prophets flourished, and so did a new literature, born out of Yiddish, the ghetto language. The Jews came out of the darkness to warm their hearts and minds in the clear sunlight of Western culture.

The new Civil Code protected the Jews' life, property, religious conscience. After fifteen hundred years, once again they had a voice in managing their own affairs. Now they could own more than the 6-by-2 plot a Jew needed to be buried in. Jews moved eagerly to taste life outside the ghetto.

But with the fall of Napoleon, the clock of Jewish emancipation was turned back. Old fences were put up again. In Germany, Jews lost their equality before the law, their political rights, their personal freedom. They could not live in rural areas, but only on the "Jew street" of the town. They had to pay special taxes on home and business. They were allowed to be only small shopkeepers, moneylenders, peddlers. Bavaria even set a quota on Jewish marriages.

The hard-pressed Bavarian Jews were the first to decide they had had enough. An America fever swept through their villages. By 1839, ten thousand Jews had left for the United States. It was the beginning of a steady migration of German-speaking Jews across the Atlantic. They came not only from Germany, but from Austria, Bohemia, Hungary, and western Poland. By 1840 the American Jewish population had risen to 15,000. Many more came after 1848, when the revolution in Germany failed and Jews lost all hope of ever winning equality there.

These newcomers, unlike the earlier wave, were poor. Many of the Spanish and Portuguese Jews had come with money and with business ties to the Old World. They prospered quickly as merchants. The German Jews had no resources and no connections. Many started in trade as peddlers, in the cities and in the countryside.

One of those pioneer peddlers was Levi Strauss. He was in his teens when he arrived from Bavaria. His brother had already opened a clothing store in New York. But Levi had his eye on California, where gold had just been discovered. He headed west with a roll of his brother's heavy denim on his back. When a miner complained that his pants wore out too quickly, Levi made him a new pair out of the canvas. The miner was so pleased he boasted all around San Francisco of his pants "from Levi's." That was the birth of Levi's, the copper-riveted pants that would last—and of a company that eventually made a jeans revolution which swept the world.

There were peddlers going west before young Strauss. The first Jew to get as far as Chicago was also a peddler, J. Gottlieb, who settled there in 1838. In a dozen years Jews replaced the old Yankee peddler who had gone up the economic ladder. Deep south they went, as far as New Orleans and Texas, and north into Michigan and Wisconsin. They traced the paths of the farmer and the hunter into the interior, lugging on their backs the household goods the settlers needed —thread, needles, hooks, ribbons, notions, stockings, underwear, cutlery. Thousands of them crisscrossed the huge continent until World War I. Many never went beyond the trade, but some found it the springboard for big business. Benjamin Altman, Adam Gimbel, Meyer Guggenheim, to name but a few, began that way. The first two founded great department stores and Guggenheim a copper kingdom.

As the factories grew, so did the peddler's stock. In the cities, peddlers had their regular stands or went door to door with pushcarts. They sold clothing, household and kitchen utensils, nuts, fruits, and candies.

Here and there, in the South and West, some peddlers settled down, opening warehouses or stores. Sons might move farther west, starting stores and giving their names to places like Gratzburg, Frankstown, Aaronsburgh. The Jewish peddler was sometimes the sole link between the settlers and the outside world, distributing news along with his wares. Frequently he might be the only Jew the settler had ever met.

The Jewish peddler (like the Yankee before him) was charged with being interested only in commerce. It was not a reasonable accusation to make. The peddler was carrying out the distribution of goods, a service just as useful and necessary as production. That profit could be made from distribution was true too of production. The two were inseparable parts of the American economic system of capitalism.

But reacting to such anti-Semitic attacks, Jews made projects to settle some of the newcomers on the land. Because they had been prevented from being farmers in feudal Europe, many Jews welcomed the chance to acquire land and farm it. No large number did, however. Poor immigrants lacked money to buy land and equipment. And if you had no experience farming, it was easier to make a living in the city. Many other Americans agreed, as the rising trend from rural to urban life showed.

In the towns and cities Jews got into many occupations. In New York among the Jews, one observer noted in 1855, "there are abundant tailors, shoemakers, tin and locksmiths, carpenters, joiners, butchers, bakers, masons, architects, and manufacturers of all kinds."

The German Jews found life favorable in a rapidly growing America. They had come poor and often uneducated, but they learned English quickly and moved up the ladder. A few became wealthy through merchandising or banking; far more ended up in the middle class, not only as shopkeepers but as lawyers, doctors, teachers, and editors.

Until the mass arrival of the Germans, the American Jews were in danger of disappearing as an ethnic group. They were few in relation to the whole population. And they were isolated from one another by distance and poor communications. Then too, unlike other immigrant groups, they came not from one country but from many, speaking different tongues, raised in different cultures. No longer under the Church's pressure to convert, they had free choice. They could maintain their Jewish loyalties, convert to another faith, or simply give up their Jewish affiliation. Many melted into the free life of the new society and lost their distinctiveness. They chose to be comfortably anonymous rather than to be an outspoken, creative minority.

But the immigrants of the new wave who came in great numbers made a stronger group life for themselves. In the larger cities they were numerous enough to support several synagogues, together with the parochial schools and charitable institutions that clustered around them. For the Jews who needed help, they provided clothing, food, fuel, bedding, loans, jobs, education, aid for the sick and the orphaned, burial services. Funds were raised by dues, contributions, banquets, concerts. By 1860 New York City had thirty-five such charitable societies, and Philadelphia twenty-three. Judah Touro of New Orleans, one of the first American philanthropists, left the then enormous sum of nearly $400,000 to both Jewish and non-Jewish causes when he died in 1854. There was little or no public welfare at the time, and such charity made a notable example for others.

The Jews as yet had found no national leadership. It was hard to unite a people living in such scattered communities. Language, custom, and class tended to separate the German Jews from the older Spanish and Portuguese Jews. But the work of devoted clergymen helped the newcomers take root in America—men like Isaac Leeser of Philadelphia, Samuel M. Isaacs of New York, Isaac M. Wise of Cincinnati, and David Einhorn of Baltimore. They had their differences, but each struggled to overcome ignorance and apathy and to strengthen Jewish life. A sense of community, an emotional bond, came to be shared by most American Jews.

This comradeship was expressed in many ways. The B'nai B'rith, founded in 1843 by German immigrants, brought Jews together for mutual aid, literary discussions, and social service. It was the first Jewish fraternal society in the world, and was organized because Jews had been turned down by other lodges.

Soon the first Jewish weekly appeared, *Israels Herold*, published in German by Isidor Bush, a refugee from the unsuccessful revolution of 1848. Its purpose was "to bring about unity among Jews," regardless of religious, political, or social differences. Other newspapers and magazines came after it, most of them edited by rabbis, at first in German, and then in English. They helped teach Judaism and Jewish history, they brought Jewish news from home and abroad, they raised funds for relief, they made dispersed Jews feel part of a community.

It was the German immigrants, especially liberal rabbis, who introduced a new cultural force, Reform Judaism. Its strongest voice, Isaac Wise, believed America offered Jews more than an open door to economic and political opportunity. He saw it as a spiritual home too, where Judaism could be relieved of the dead weight of tradition and the strangling hand of reactionary government.

As they rose into the American middle class, Jews wanted to adapt to its ways. Earlier, in Germany, the reform movement had stemmed from the same impulse. Jews of higher social standing had wanted to modernize the traditional services and traditional Jewish education. Passionate followers of reason, they took a fresh look at the old regulations that had grown up around Judaism over long centuries. They wanted a Judaism fitted for life in the modern world. In America, said Rabbi Wise, the Jew needed to be freed from tradition so that his going out into the world would not necessarily mean deserting Judaism.

Looking to the prophets, the Reformers found the cornerstone for the new Judaism. Judaism had a special mission in the world, they said—to strive for the well-being of all mankind. It was the ideal proclaimed by the Hebrew prophets— social justice. As a progressive religion, Judaism could change its form with the advance of knowledge.

The Reformers were opposed by the Orthodox—the upholders of traditional Judaism. Change any form, practice, or law, the Orthodox argued, and where would the challenge to divine sanction stop? Judaism is what tradition has made it, they said, or it is nothing.

Reform Judaism made headway, winning a large following. But when the next great wave of Jewish immigration came, in the 1880s, Orthodox Judaism was greatly strengthened by the eastern Europeans. A third movement, Conservative Judaism, came into being later as an attempt to achieve a compromise between the other two. But no single organization has ever been able to embrace all Jews and every strand of Judaism in America.

In the decades before the Civil War, Jews began moving farther west. By 1850 there were two hundred families in Chicago, more than enough to open the city's first synagogue. Some of them were Democrats, some Whigs, and a few Free-Soilers. They were friendly with the Christians, mixing in political and social clubs and in the volunteer fire department. "Prejudices, if not dead, are at least hidden," said one Chicagoan. For entertainment there were carriage rides and walks in the fields during the summer, and sleigh rides, theater parties, and dances in the winter. Sunday was visiting day. The Jews were in many businesses and trades; none were rich but most were able to live in modest one- or two-story frame houses.

The Gold Rush lured many Jews, besides young Levi Strauss, to the Far West. They opened trading posts on the plains and in the mountains. By the end of the 1850s Jewish communities had sprung up in many western towns, the largest of them in San Francisco.

One Jew helped pioneer the land route to the West. He was Solomon Nunes Carvalho, a Charleston artist and photographer who in 1854 served as staff photographer on John C. Frémont's fifth expedition across the Rocky Mountains.

By 1860, America's Jewish population had grown to some 150,000. Two out of three of them were immigrants. Most Americans probably never thought about the Jews.

Nevertheless, anti-Semitism persisted here as it had for a much longer time in the rest of the world. An individual would be abused as a Jew by someone who envied or opposed him. Jews who achieved prominence in whatever field were likely to suffer attacks upon their origins or faith, even those who had long ago abandoned Judaism to become Christians. But attacks upon Jews *as a people* were rare.

One important reason, of course, was that Jews were still a tiny minority in America. The Know-Nothing movement, for instance, ignored the Jews. The far more numerous Irish Catholic immigrants took the brunt of violent attacks upon the "vicious and ignorant outsiders" whom the nativists called a threat to American democracy.

As early as 1832 the charge was made that politically Jews voted as a bloc. Denying they wished to be represented in office as a religious group, eighty-four Jews of Charleston, S.C., stated their views in a letter to the press. Like other Americans, Jews were divided along social, political, and economic lines. "We will not support any man for office who is not selected by the public for himself, his character, and his talents," they said.

The fact that Jews could win popular confidence is clear in the number elected to public office. Among them were a governor of Georgia, four U.S. representatives, and two U.S. senators—Louisiana's Judah P. Benjamin, and David Yulee of Florida.

Jews felt optimistic about their future in a land that guaranteed full civil and political rights to all. To all? To all but another, far larger minority, whose skins were black. The issue of slavery was bringing America to a tragic crisis about to explode in armed conflict. Jews would learn they had to fight for acceptance in a war to enlarge the boundaries of human freedom.

Chapter 4

SLAVERY AND CIVIL WAR

"Man—thus reads the doctrine of Sinai—is created in the image of God, and, as such, born free . . . He may belong to this or that race; he is God's servant . . . but never the 'slave' or the property of man . . . The spirit of Judaism demands the abolition of slavery."

It took courage for Rabbi David Einhorn to voice that belief in Baltimore, the heart of a slave state. But the Bavarian immigrant had learned at home what loss of freedom meant. When he came to Baltimore in 1855 as Reform Rabbi, at once he urged the destruction of slavery as "the cancer of the union." He saw the connection between the rights of the Jew and the rights of the black. How could any minority feel secure in a country which accepted the enslavement of any people?

Slavery was the issue splitting America. To be opposed to "the peculiar institution" was to join the cause of freedom, the side of progress. There were many Jews who made that choice. And also Jews who took the other side, the side of reaction. Both sides—abolitionist and pro-slavery—marshaled Scripture to support their position. So too the Christians, who used the Bible to give religious sanction to their stand. Whether Jew or non-Jew, a man's position on such a basic issue had less to do with his religion than with his class, regional, political, or racial interests as he saw them.

It was that way from the beginning. Pious Christians and pious Jews, among them the "best people" of the colonies, took part in the slave trade. For the first two hundred years of American slavery only a handful of white Americans questioned its morality. The Cabots, the Waldos, the Royalls, the Browns, the Pepperrells, the Crowninshields—those most prestigious families of New England drew their wealth largely from slavery. So did Aaron Lopez of Newport.

In the old South the typical Jew was a peddler or small storekeeper. Few Jews were planters. Jews who became prosperous enough were likely to own slaves, as did the general society. But few in number as they were, Jews never played a major role in the business of slavery.

Some southern Jews did not accept the exploitation of slaves. In most cases they took only personal action on their views, refusing to own slaves. Judah Touro of New Orleans was said to have bought slaves solely to free them. The Friedmann brothers of Alabama helped the slave Peter Still to evade a state law against emancipation by taking him North. But most southern Jews went along with the ways of the slave society.

In the North, where the Jewish community was considerably larger, its leaders spoke out—on both sides of the question. But they never claimed an official voice. The Anti-Slavery Society had hoped that as victims of prejudice and oppression over the ages, Jews would take a united stand against slavery. But the Jews had no single religious body to speak for them. As the Charleston Jews had said on another occasion, they believed the Jewish citizen should take whatever position he thought best for his own interests and his country's welfare. The abolitionists had no better luck when they tried to swing Christian denominations behind them. Indeed, almost until the beginning of the Civil War, the name abolitionist was a name of disgrace.

Nevertheless, Jews as individuals were active in the struggle against slavery. As early as 1806 Moses Judah, a New York merchant, took leadership in a society working to liberate the slaves. Jews like Michael Greenebaum of Chicago, who opposed the Fugitive Slave Law of 1850, aided runaways to escape in defiance of the law. August Bondi, another veteran of

the 1848 revolution in Europe, fought with John Brown's
guerrillas in the struggle to make the Kansas Territory a free
state. Isidor Bush and Moritz Pinner were leaders of the
abolitionist movement in Missouri. And one of the greatest
anti-slavery orators was Ernestine Rose, daughter of a Polish
rabbi. From 1836 on she traveled all through the North and
West to rally support for abolition as well as for women's
rights.

In April 1861 southern guns fired on Fort Sumter to begin
the Civil War. The *Jewish Messenger* called upon Jews "to
rally as one man for the Union and the Constitution." The
editor, Rabbi Samuel M. Isaacs of New York, championed the
Union cause as "the side of liberty and justice."

In Baltimore, Rabbi Einhorn urged every northern Jew to
support the Union. "Who has more at stake," he asked, "con-
cerning the question whether freedom or slavery ought to
become the basis of our state life than our brethren, who
today in most of the lands of the old world still languish
under slavery?" When a pro-slavery mob rioted in the city's
streets, hunting down friends of the Union, he was forced to
flee to Philadelphia.

Jews answered at once to Lincoln's call for troops. More
than six thousand served in the Union Army. Eleven reached
the rank of general. Typical was Frederick Knefler, Hungarian
immigrant, who rose from private to colonel of the 79th In-
diana Infantry, and then was promoted to brigadier general
for gallant and meritorious service. Jewish soldiers earned
seven Congressional Medals of Honor.

Chicago's Jewish community of a thousand recruited and
financed among themselves an infantry company of 96 men
in two days. Syracuse quickly contributed a Jewish company.
But most Jews served in mixed units. They would rather give
up religious observances, such as dietary laws, than fight in
segregated units. The same was true on the Confederate
side, which 1500 Jews joined.

Soon after fighting began, Congress passed a law providing
that all military chaplains must be Christian ministers. A

congressman's protest that this would be discriminating against Jews was ignored. Jews speedily pressured Congress to change the law, and won their case. Jacob Frankel of Philadelphia became the first American rabbi to be appointed a military chaplain.

A little earlier, in 1860, Congress had recognized the equal status of Judaism with Christianity as an American faith by inviting Rabbi Morris J. Raphall of New York to open a House session with prayer. (It was this same rabbi who soon after gave a sermon justifying slavery as in accord with God's will, as set forth in the Bible.)

While their men shed their blood to end slavery, Jewish families strengthened the cause with service on the home front. Their synagogues, welfare societies, and social clubs gave their energies to war aid, preparing bandages, raising funds for the relief of soldiers' families, sending food and clothing to the wounded, helping in hospitals. One major action was to convert several wards of the Jews' Hospital in New York for military use. The hospital, founded in 1852 and later renamed Mount Sinai, had given American Jews the first medical facility they could call their own, a modern one staffed by able Jewish and non-Jewish doctors. Now it volunteered complete care for wounded soldiers, only a small number of whom would be Jewish.

The funds Jews contributed to the Union cause were considerable. The New York banker Joseph Seligman raised $200,000,000 selling Union bonds in Germany—an achievement the historian William E. Dodd called "scarcely less important than the Battle of Gettysburg" because it won for Lincoln the financial and diplomatic banking he desperately needed at this point.

Still, with all their contribution of blood and treasure to the war effort, Jews felt a tide of prejudice lapping higher and higher around them. Men like Seligman were called "the Jew banker" in the press and charged with "betraying the country" to "enrich the whole tribe of Jews."

Any vast social upheaval such as war releases hidden or

sleeping prejudices. North and South were convulsed with pain, fear, anger, suffering, frustration, hatred, grief. The Jews became one of the escape valves for all those pent-up feelings. Many made the Jews scapegoats for the hurt and harm suffered during the war. For the Jews it was the heaviest barrage of prejudice ever directed against them in America.

Because there were Jewish soldiers serving the Confederacy, and one of its leaders was Judah Benjamin, some northern papers charged the Jews were all unpatriotic. *Harper's Weekly,* for instance, printed pieces saying all Jews were secessionists, Copperheads, and rebels. What could the "Christ-killers" be but traitors, was a theme editors repeatedly stressed. Jews who enlisted in the Union Army or were reported wounded in action were never identified as Jews in the press. But let any be accused of wrongdoing, and he was instantly labeled "Jew."

Several leading military and political figures on the North's side made their prejudices public. Generals Benjamin Butler and William T. Sherman, Senators Henry Wilson and Andrew Johnson, Colonel LaFayette Baker, head of the Secret Service, were among them.

The most notorious anti-Semitic episode of the war revolved around General U. S. Grant. In 1862, as commander of the Department of the Tennessee, he issued his infamous Order No. 11, expelling all Jews from the region. Hordes of speculators had descended on the region to make huge profits out of cotton. They had corrupted army officers through bribery and secret partnerships in their illegal operations. Some of the profiteers were Jews: most were not. But Grant's order blamed the "Jews as a class." Without trial or hearing, he ordered them all—men, women, and children—to get out within twenty-four hours. So sweeping an anti-Jewish regulation had long been suffered by Jews abroad, but had never been known here. Among those subject to the order were thirty Jewish families of Paducah, Kentucky. Unable to reach Grant, they wired President Lincoln protesting "this inhuman order" which would violate Jews' rights as citizens and make them appear "outlaws before the whole world." When no response came, their spokesman, Cesar Kaskel, went to Washington, D.C., to present the true facts to Lincoln. Meanwhile the national capital was bombarded with protests from Jews all over the North. The President listened to Kaskel and at once had the order revoked. Shortly after, to a delegation of Cincinnati Jews who thanked him, he said, "To condemn a class is, to say the least, to wrong the good with the bad. I do not like to hear a class or nationality condemned on account of a few sinners."

The Republican press and politicians failed to come to the Jews' defense. Shocked and pained by the government's offense, Jews were angered by this added failure to wipe out the shame. Nevertheless, they continued to support the Union cause.

In the South, too, anti-Jewish feelings mounted as the war dragged on. And when defeat seemed certain, the Jews were blamed for the failure of the Confederacy. A New Orleans journalist called for the Jews to be "exterminated." Judah Benjamin, already a target for northern bigots, now was denounced as the "Judas Iscariot" of the Confederacy.

The Jews, of course, led the fight against prejudice, through their journals and by protest meetings. They did not remain silent in the face of slander. Some non-Jewish editors came to their support, crying out for a halt to Jew-baiting. But such defenders were few. Jews could only hope that with the end of war, the tide of intolerance would recede.

Chapter 5

POVERTY AND POGROMS

This Sunday they were sure the Tsar would die. Six times before, the young terrorists in the revolutionary party "The People's Will" had tried to assassinate the ruler of Russia. Every attempt had failed; it had cost them twenty-one executions. Now they had to hurry. The police were moving toward the center of their secret organization. If we succeed, the revolutionaries told themselves, the people will rise up and remake Russia into a democratic society.

They had studied closely the habits of Alexander II. Every Sunday in St. Petersburg the Tsar did the same thing. He walked or drove to the Catherine Canal. The terrorist cell made plans to bomb him on his route. Four men volunteered to do the job under the command of Sophya Perovskaya. It was a suicide mission: the bomb each man held was designed for throwing at close range.

On Sunday, March 1, 1881, the watching Sophya waved a white handkerchief to warn her comrades stationed along the Catherine Canal. The signal meant the Tsar's sledge was in sight. As the sledge drew alongside him, the first man flung his bomb. The explosion smashed the sledge, wounded some in the royal procession, but did not injure the Tsar. Then it was the turn of the second man to hurl his bomb. It killed both himself and the Tsar.

The plot was a success.

But though the Tsar was dead, there was no popular uprising. Peasants, workers, students—they were shocked, stunned,

but they did nothing. Swiftly the police captured the con-
spirators. After a trial, they were hanged.

With the murder of Alexander II, his son came into power.
And Alexander III, who believed his father had been too
liberal, released all the terrors of the night.

It was a bloody disaster especially for Russia's Jews. Anti-
Semitism was a strong tradition in Russia long before this
new Tsar came to the throne. Jews had lived in eastern Europe
since the thirteenth century, when a Polish King had invited
them in. He wanted to encourage commercial growth in a
peasant society. The settlers became traders, stewards, innkeepers, moneylenders, tax collectors, artisans, grain merchants.
Proving themselves essential to the economy, many Jews rose
into the middle class.

In the eighteenth century Poland was invaded by Cossacks,
Swedes, and Russians. The country broke into pieces that
stronger neighbors grabbed. The majority of Jews fell under
Russian rule. They were treated even worse than the Russian
peasants, held in bondage to their masters for centuries. The
Jews, who had never before been allowed to live in Russia,
were now penned up in the provinces of western and south-
western Russia, an area called the Pale of Settlement.

As though isolation in a great ghetto were not enough, the
Jews were humiliated and hounded by hundreds of restrictions.
Russian officials forced out innkeepers, renters, middlemen.
They expelled Jews from village after village. They tried to
make Jews quit commerce and trade for farming. Assigned to
remote, desolate lands, unprepared and ill-equipped, many
Jewish peasants starved and died.

Military conscription was one of the heaviest burdens piled
upon the Jews. From the 1820s Jewish boys of twelve had been
drafted. For the first six years in service the Tsar tried to
Russify them, to turn them away from Judaism under the guise
of military training. Then they had to endure twenty-five more
years of army service. The Jewish communities were given
army quotas to fill. Later, the law took away that choice of
which Jews were to serve. All Jews reaching twenty-one had

to enter the Army for twenty-five years, and no Jew could be promoted above private. Boys stole across the border and fled overseas to escape the draft.

In the 1860s Alexander II emancipated the serfs and introduced other liberal measures. For a few privileged Jews the vise of the Pale was loosened. Some prospered and were permitted to live in the great cities—Moscow, St. Petersburg, Kiev. But in the 1870s controls were again clamped tight. The Jews felt themselves adrift on a dangerous sea, buffeted by waves of hostility from local officials, landowners, and peasants. Whatever the Russian people suffered—poverty, hunger, misfortune —was always blamed on the Jews.

So too was the murder of Alexander II. "The Jews did it." This false charge was heard everywhere. A pogrom—the organized massacre of helpless people—broke out in Elisavetgrad. The wild riots spread to Odessa and Kiev. Tens of thousands of Jews were injured or killed in 1881–82. Pogroms were the Tsar's lightning rod. He could divert attention from his government's mistakes and failures by encouraging acts of violence against the Jews.

Already there were 650 restrictive laws in force against the Jews. Now the government added new ones. The May Laws barred Jews from owning or renting land outside the towns or cities. Jews were discouraged from living in villages. Quotas were set to keep Jews out of schools and universities. Jews could not practice law or take part in local elections. Year after year, there were more such suffocating laws. Jews allowed to live in the big cities outside the Pale because there was a practical need for them were abruptly cast out. Thus 14,000 Jewish artisans were brutally driven out of Moscow. The liquor trade was made a government monopoly and thousands of Jews running inns and restaurants lost their livelihood.

Jews starved in the slums. A Vilna newspaper described their condition:

> They live in miserable hovels . . . Filth is everywhere—inside and out. In the same dwelling may be

found four, five, even six families, each of them having a number of children of tender age. To add to the misery, neither beds, nor chairs, nor tables are to be seen in the wretched hovels, but everyone has to lie on the damp and infected ground. Meat is an unknown luxury, even on the Sabbath. Today bread and water, tomorrow water and bread, and so on day after day.

The four million Jews in Russia became a driven, desperate people. Little better off were the Jews in Galicia and Bukovina, the easternmost provinces of the Austro-Hungarian Empire. How could the Jews escape oppression? Where could they go to find freedom and equality?

Thousands left their homeland forever. In the thirty years following Alexander's assassination, one out of every three Jews in eastern Europe said goodbye to their country. It was a mass flight from poverty and persecution.

Most of them came to America. The first group to reach New York was 250 Jews who arrived on July 29, 1881, only three months after the first pogrom at Elisavetgrad.

Imagine how hard it must have been for poor people living in remote villages of eastern Europe to cross a continent and an ocean to reach a strange new land. Used to hardship as they were, the natural tendency was to stay put. To visit even the next province was something many people never did. Those unable to read or write had only the vaguest idea where Moscow was, much less far-off New York.

Still, a small number of the more adventurous had all these years been making the crossing. Their letters from America brought news of how different life could be. "Cobbler and teacher have the same title—Mister," wrote one girl, "and all the children, boys and girls, Jews and Gentiles, go to school!"

Then too, the mere sight of a man here, a family there, picking up and departing for America—that was something to stir you out of your rut and make you think. As for the excitement when an immigrant returned to bring others to the

New World! Friends and relations would pour into such a family's house, day and night, to meet the returned one and hear the wonders of his story.

The vision they held out of the Goldeneh Medina—the Golden Land—fascinated their listeners. Anzia Yezierska, whose childhood was lived in Russia, remembered it:

> In America you can say what you feel—you can voice your thoughts in the open streets without fear of a Cossack. In America is a home for everybody. The land is your land. Not like in Russia where you feel yourself a stranger in the village where you were born and raised—the village in which your father and grandfather lie buried . . . Everybody is with everybody alike in America. Christians and Jews are brothers together . . . An end to the worry for bread. An end to the fear of the bosses over you. Everybody can do what he wants with his life in America . . . There are no high or low in America. Even the President holds hands with Gedalyeh Mindel. Plenty for all. Learning flows free like milk and honey.

Once the desire to go yourself was awakened, how to do it? Where to go? How to get there? What would it cost? The immigrants had to pack pots and pans, bedding and samovar, say goodbye to loved ones, perhaps forever, then find their way to the ports of western Europe. By 1880 steam had largely displaced sail, and the price of steerage passage might run from $12 to $35, including food (a sum that sounds small today, but was bigger than many Jews earned the year round). The immigrants who crossed in the 1840s were often forty days at sea. The new ships cut it to three weeks or less.

The old-style steerage was still widely used. The shipping lines wanted to carry the greatest possible number in the smallest possible space. On one German ship, the *Amerika,* the 220 upper-class passengers traveled in four-berth cabins, with a dining room to hold them in two seatings. The mass of

passengers—2000 of them—were distributed on three decks.
They slept in double-decker iron beds, with straw mattresses
and no pillows. The very low partitions gave them no privacy.
For the 2000 in steerage there were forty toilets and sixty
washbasins, and two 20-foot-square galleys, each with a tiny
kosher kitchen attached. There was no dining space, and no
public rooms to relax in. Photos from those years show women
and children sitting on ladders or pipes, and great crowds
standing shoulder to shoulder on the decks.

A journalist crossing on one such ship reported the food
consisted of "mugs of celery soup . . . not a chunk of bread
less than an inch thick, the hash of gristly beef and warm
potatoes that would not have been tolerated in the poorest
restaurant." He noted that the eastern Europeans gulped
everything down anyhow. They lined up with their mess tins
outside the galley, ate on the open deck, and washed up in
cold sea water, with no soap or towels provided.

Abraham Cahan, a Russian immigrant, described the experience in his novel *The Rise of David Levinsky:*

> Who can depict the feeling of desolation, home-
> sickness, uncertainty, and anxiety with which an emi-
> grant makes his first voyage across the ocean? I proved
> to be a good sailor, but the sea frightened me. The
> thumping of the engines was drumming a ghastly
> accompaniment to the awesome whisper of the waves.
> I felt in the embrace of a vast, uncanny force. And
> echoing through it all were the heart-lashing words:
> "Are you crazy? You forget your place, young man!"

And when the immigrants at last caught sight of the America
they had dreamed about? Anzia Yezierska told how they felt:

> Land! Land! came the joyous shout. America!
> We're in America! cried my mother, almost smother-
> ing us in her rapture. All crowded and pushed on
> deck. They strained and stretched to get the first

glimpse of the golden country, lifting their children on their shoulders so that they might see beyond them. Men fell on their knees to pray. Women hugged their babies and wept. Children danced. Strangers embraced and kissed like old friends. Old men and women had in their eyes a look of young people in love. Age-old visions sang themselves in me—songs of freedom of an oppressed people. America—America.

In the 1880s, the gateway for immigrants was Castle Garden, a former opera house at the southern tip of Manhattan. Then the federal Immigration Bureau took over in 1892 and made Ellis Island in New York harbor the place for inspecting and caring for the immigrants.

Here, in the red brick buildings, the weary newcomers were put through a puzzling maze that could drag on for days. Officials studied their papers, looked into their eyes and their throats, listened to their hearts, made entries on cards, and pinned tags to their coats. Then came the questions—where are you bound for, what money do you have, who are your relatives, is there a job waiting for you?

For many immigrants Ellis Island, the portal to America, was made a horror by officialdom. Not until they arrived were they told they needed to have $25 to be admitted to America. If they could not produce it, they were sent home. To call attention to their plight a hundred immigrants signed a letter that was printed on page one of the *Forward*:

We are packed into a room where there is space for two hundred people, but they have crammed in about a thousand. They don't let us out into the yard for a little fresh air. We lie about on the floor in the spittle and the filth. We're wearing the same shirts for three or four weeks, because we don't have our baggage with us.

Everyone goes around dejected and cries and wails. Women with little babies, who have come to their

husbands, are being detained. Who can stand this
suffering? Men are separated from their wives and
children and only when they take us out to eat can
they see them. When a man wants to ask his wife
something, or when a father wants to see his child,
they don't let him. Children get sick, they are taken
to a hospital, and it often happens that they never
come back . . .

Tuesday they begin again to lead us to the "slaughter," that is, to the boat. And God knows how many
Jewish lives this will cost, because more than one mind
dwells on the thought of jumping into the water when
they take him to the boat . . .

The week before, 600 detained immigrants had been sent
back. The day this letter was published, 270 more were sent
back.

In 1882, Russian immigration jumped to 21,000—about 70
per cent of it Jewish. By 1890 it rose to 35,000. And as Russian
oppression of Jews intensified, the exodus swelled. In the fifty
years from 1880 to 1930, the migration of European Jews
would increase the size of the American Jewish community
from 250,000 to 3,500,000.

Who were the new Jews? They were only a small fraction of
all the immigrants pouring into America. Second, they were a
minority of the Jews from among whom they came. Two thirds
of the eastern European Jews remained where they were, de-
spite poverty and persecution. And third, they were poor.

So poor, that over half had no money at all. The average
amount Jews entered with was $15.50, as against the general
immigrant average of $22. That they were able to come at all
was thanks to relatives who in two thirds of the cases supplied
the passage money.

Unlike the German Jews who had come before them, many
were workers. Seven out of ten were artisans—the largest proportion for any immigrant group. Half were in the needle
trades. The others included tanners, furriers, blacksmiths,

cobblers, tinsmiths, hatmakers, carpenters, butchers, bakers, watchmakers.

A fourth of the Jewish immigrants were illiterate. Respect for learning was an ancient tradition, but they had been denied schooling so long they reached America with this too as a handicap.

The earlier Sephardic and German immigrants had come from highly developed countries. They had a good secular as well as Jewish education. Experienced in commerce and finance, many had risen rapidly in business, especially in the retail trades. Altman's, Stern's, Macy's, Bloomingdale's, Saks, Gimbels—the modern department stores grew out of German Jewish energy and imagination.

The eastern Europeans, by contrast, came from backward and even feudal countries. They knew something of traditional Jewish culture, but had little or no other education, for middle- and upper-class Jews did not emigrate. The newcomers found the frontier settled, and for the most part stayed in the big cities. Perhaps 90 per cent made New York their home.

Until the 1870s there had been no distinct Jewish quarter in New York. The Jews from central Europe had settled in what was chiefly a German and Irish neighborhood. This was the Lower East Side of Manhattan. The wholesale and retail businesses run by the German Jews and the garment trade which they dominated ran along Grand Street and Canal Street. It was this neighborhood into which the east European immigrants began coming.

Chapter 6

ON THE LOWER EAST SIDE

Call the roll of streets—Hester, Stanton, Forsyth, Cherry, Essex, Norfolk, Ludlow, Mott, Crosby, Baxter, Bayard—and almost every American Jew whose roots go back to east Europe will recognize a way station in family history. By the early 1900s the Lower East Side had become a sea of Jewish immigrants. (The middle-class Germans and Irish had retreated to less crowded neighborhoods.) It was the most densely packed part of New York as factories and shops jammed in next to crowded tenements. The district, said one visitor, "seemed to sweat humanity at every window and door."

Along block after block run the six-to-eight-story tenements, their fronts lined with fire escapes, the streets below with pushcarts and peddlers. The customers bargain in Yiddish—tin cups for 2 cents, peaches a penny a quart, hats for a quarter, spectacles for 35 cents, a pair of pants for 30 cents, a single egg, an ounce of tea, a quarter of a chicken, an overripe tomato . . . millions of suspenders.

Jostle your way through the crowd, weaving in and out of counters made of planks laid across boards, stumbling over boxes of goods piled on the sidewalk, and go into any tenement. This one is seven stories high. The hallway is smelly and dark, so dark you cannot see your hand and need to feel your way to the stairs. Up on the first landing you find a hallway with two toilets, a sink, and a cold-water tap. At each end are two apartments of four rooms. Some of the rooms have windows on the street or the foul-smelling air shaft, others

In the early 1900s many Jewish immigrants settled in the Lower East Side. The market place was lined with

pushcarts and peddlers where food and clothing was
sold.

have none at all, and a visiting nurse needs to light a candle to see her patient. The tiny apartment you drop into—no room longer than 11 feet—houses a "family" of father, mother, twelve children, and six boarders. With more than thirty such families in a single tenement, it is no wonder a square mile on the Lower East Side packs in 330,000 people.

In case of fire, these tenements are deathtraps, for who could escape by the narrow stairway or the flimsy fire escape littered with junk? Relentless summer heat converts the roof, the fire escape, the sidewalk into sleeping quarters.

Look about the tiny flat and you wonder, where can clothes be hung? Where can things be stored? Where can children play? Where can a father home from work find room to rest and quiet to restore himself? The rats rustling in the cellar, the bugs crawling on the walls, the noise from the street, the stink from the garbage, these too are part of everyday life.

Crowding and dirt inevitably make for sickness and crime. East European Jews came here physically stunted by centuries of ghetto life and poverty. Yet in the American slums they suffered less from contagious disease than other immigrant groups. The strict sanitary laws of Orthodox Jewry made many cook their food properly, clean up the house at least one day of the week, and go to the public baths regularly. Still, many Jews fell victim to tuberculosis. Diabetes too took its toll, as did mental illness caused by the harshness and insecurity of this strange new life. Suicides were not many, perhaps because of the strong ties to family and community. But unable to make it, large numbers of men deserted their families.

The Lower East Side, like the slums everywhere, generated crime and violence, committed not by the immigrant generation, but by the next. "It is not until they have been Americanized, have adapted themselves to the environment of the district and adopted its ways and vices, that they become full-fledged wretches," said one observer, Dr. I. L. Nascher.

The way the slums could poison the spirit was caught in a song written by Morris Rosenfeld, one of the poets of the Lower East Side:

I lift mine eyes against the sky,
The clouds are weeping, so am I.
I lift mine eyes again on high,
The sun is smiling, so am I.
Why do I smile? Why do I weep?
I do not know; it lies too deep.

I hear the winds of autumn sigh,
They break my heart, they make me cry.
I hear the birds of lovely spring,
My hopes revive, I help them sing.
Why do I sing? Why do I cry?
It lies so deep, I know not why.

Was life in America any worse for Jews than for other immigrants? Some argue it was. A Norwegian farmer could go to the Dakotas or Minnesota to farm, much as he had in his native land. A German craftsman could use his skill in Milwaukee the way he had in Munich. A Polish miner could dig coal or iron in the Alleghenies just as he had in the Carpathians. But for the Jew from eastern Europe who had lived in the shtetl, nothing had prepared him for the pushcart or sweatshop life he would experience in American ghettos.

Even the disaster of being without work had different meaning in America. Here it was no work, no eat, as this letter from an unemployed man shows. Years before he had deserted from the Russian Army and fled to America. He writes to the *Jewish Daily Forward*:

I am an ironworker. I can work a milling machine and a drill press. I can also drive horses and train colts. I have been jobless for six months now, I have eaten the last shirt on my back and now there is nothing left for me but to end my life. I have struggled long enough in the dark world. Death is better than such a life. One goes about with strong hands, one wants to sell them for a bit of bread, and no one

wants to buy. They tell you coldbloodedly: "We don't
need you." Can you imagine how heartsick one gets?

I get up at four in the morning to hunt a job
through the newspaper. I have no money for carfare,
so I go on foot, but by the time I get to the place there
are hundreds before me. Then I run wherever my eyes
lead me. Lately I've spent five cents a day on food,
and the last two days I don't have even that. I have
no strength to go on . . . If I had known it would be
so bitter for me here, I wouldn't have come. I didn't
come here for a fortune, but where is bread? What can
I do now?

There, in the shtetl, the Jewish family might have a garden,
a little strip of land, maybe a cow, hens. They could often
borrow flour or potatoes from a neighbor till the next harvest.
Unemployment didn't always mean starvation in that simple
economy.

But neither could you make money in the shtetl. In America,
it was said, you could go from rags to riches. Andrew Carnegie
—there was proof. Hadn't he started from the bottom and
become one of the world's wealthiest men? Carnegies there
were, but the truth was, there was little room at the top if you
didn't come from the right family, with money and education.
That didn't mean there wasn't plenty of room below that
pinnacle. So with infinitely greater chances of success here,
the newcomers pitched headlong into the fierce struggle to
make it.

You could go in by many routes. The lowly pushcart was
one. You could see 1500 peddlers any day in the neighborhood of Hester, Norfolk, and Essex streets. A license was $25
a year plus small bribes to the cops. The peddler rarely earned
more than $5 a week so he often hired a pushcart for his
wife, and sometimes his children too. The shop on wheels
could be rented for 10 cents a day and filled with stuff from
Canal Street wholesalers. Bargains, bargains, bargains. Everything had to go in a hurry—the whole load of secondhand

goods in one day, for there was no place to store leftovers. A step above the pushcart was the customer-peddler. He went door to door taking orders for goods. And if a family could get together the capital, they could move on up another step, opening a store of their own, living in back, and working in the front. Work began when the sun rose and ended late at night, when the last customer drifted out. "The only schedule was money," wrote the poet Harry Roskolenko, "and that had no clock at all. It was a blueprint in the head, hands, stomach, and ears."

This was retailing. Another route was manufacturing. And this usually meant getting into the garment trades. Producing ready-made clothing for the masses was a new business. It took little capital to start. It offered jobs for the east European Jews, or the chance to become a man of business for those who could scrape up the money.

Arriving at a boom time of industrialization, the Jewish immigrants moved into unskilled and semiskilled jobs, especially in the light industry springing up on the Lower East Side. They knew no English and with no funds, settled for work in the garment industry, the tobacco and cigar trades, or household goods. Their religious and social needs rooted them to the spot where their kinsmen lived.

Leaders of the middle-class German Jewish community were distressed by the ignorance, poverty, and crudity of the east Europeans. They tried to direct the newcomers west, to other cities or to agricultural labor. Nor did they want to see the immigrants become competitors or burdens. Some Jews were eager to try farming, which eastern Europe generally had shut them out of. They went to self-help agricultural colonies started by philanthropists. About three thousand families took part in the colonization movement. But it did not succeed. The vast majority of Jews did not go back to the soil. They felt more at home in the cities.

"At home?" In New York, that came to mean for countless thousands life in a sweatshop. The "sweating system" was the name for the way ready-made clothing was manufactured in the tenements of the Lower East Side. Between the manufacturer and the worker there now were middlemen, called contractors. The manufacturer cut and bunched materials for each garment. Then he distributed them in large lots to the contractors, each a specialist in his line. One made cloaks, another coats, another pants, and some made special grades or sizes. A few contractors did the work in lofts but most in their homes. Because work was irregular they hired help at a daily shape-up on the corner of Hester and Ludlow, called the "Pig Market." The workers lugged their own sewing machines to the market and then to the site of the job. Other contractors sublet their work to a "sweater" who also did the job in his home, with his family as the labor.

After investigating these sweatshops, a congressional committee concluded in 1893 that "A large proportion of all the clothing worn by the majority of our people is made under conditions revolting to humanity and decency."

The reporter Jacob Riis, in his book *How the Other Half Lives*, pictured the sweatshops:

> The homes of the Hebrew quarter are its workshops also. You are made fully aware of it before you have travelled the length of a single block in any of these East Side streets, by the whir of a thousand sewing machines, worked at high pressure from earliest dawn till mind and muscle give out together. Every member of the family, from the youngest to the oldest, bears a hand, shut in the qualmy rooms, where meals are cooked and clothing washed and dried besides, the live-long day. It is not unusual to find a dozen persons—men, women and children—at work in a single small room.

Then Riis takes us into a Ludlow Street tenement:

> Five men and a woman, two young girls, not fifteen, and a boy who says unasked that he is fifteen, and lies in saying it, are at the machines sewing knicker-

Many Jewish people used their homes as workshops.
The women would stitch up the clothes on sewing machines, while the men cut the patterns.

bockers . . . The floor is littered ankle-deep with half-sewn garments. In the alcove, on a couch of many dozens of pants ready for the finisher, a bare-legged baby with pinched face is asleep. A fence of piled-up clothing keeps him from rolling off on the floor. The faces, hands and arms to the elbows of everyone in the room are black with the color of the cloth on which they are working.

An investigation showed that in 1907 there were 60,000 children shut up in these home sweatshops. Many of them had never sat on a school bench. The poet Edwin Markham went out to see what "this nerve-racking work of our hurried age" was doing to the children:

> Nearly any hour on the East Side of New York City you can see them—pallid boy or spindling girl —their faces dulled, their backs bent under a heavy load of garments piled on head and shoulders, the muscles of the whole frame in a long strain. The boy always has bowlegs and walks with feet wide apart and wobbling . . . Once at home with the sewing, the little worker sits close to the inadequate window, struggling with the snarls of thread or shoving the needle through unyielding cloth . . . Never again should one complain of buttons hanging by a thread, for tiny, tortured fingers have doubtless done their little ineffectual best. And for his lifting of burdens, this giving of youth and strength, this sacrifice of all that should make childhood radiant, a child may add to the family purse from 50 cents to $1.50 a week.

It fused into one huge ugliness, an "inhuman zoo," one garment worker said. He was Harry Roskolenko's father. One day young Harry visited the factory to bring his father a letter from Russia and an apple. Years later Harry recalled what he saw:

It was just an ordinary shop, I discovered, with nothing special about the men, the work, heat, the dirt, the pay, the boss, the production. It was a factory with a hundred workers stripped down to their pants. All sorts of tailoring, cutting, and pressing machines were whirling, whirring and steaming away. I was fascinated for a few minutes—then I saw my father. I lost the magic of a new place at once. The inventions were gone, and there was a man of fifty, pressing a cloak with a ten-pound steam iron . . .

It was summer sweat, winter sweat, all sorts of sweat: bitter, sour, stinking, moldy—through all the seasons of the year. Not one fan to blow up some wind. The fans were in the boss's office . . . Instead of fans there were foremen walking about, fuming and blowing, their voices like dogs barking at other dogs. The workers seldom paused, no matter what they were at . . . And no one smoked except during lunch or when a worker went to the toilet. They were watched there as well . . . How long to urinate, how long to move your bowels? Nothing in nature took very long over piecework or the need to produce downtown what was needed uptown at the end of the day or that afternoon . . . With this system of sweating, every worker gave up his lunchtime—the minutes saved, to earn a bit more. Eat faster or eat less. Or eat what took no time at all—and then back to the steam and the machines, and to the *gontser macher* barking to his dogs.

The day began in the dark, too early for sun's rising, and it ended in the dark, too late for sun's setting. It was 12 hours, 14 hours, 16, depending on what the worker needed at home . . . Yes, what was needed at home? What was not? Who was coming over from Poland, Russia, Hungary—another relative? How much did the *shifskart* (steamship ticket) cost? And the money might or might not be paid back. Another

pogrom, too . . . and my father had read the letter.
It was a simple appeal—*Save me* . . . and more hours
were put in that week, that month . . . hours beyond
reckoning. It was a death-ridden loft making a young
man middle-aged and the middle-aged ancient. The
skin changed daily, the lungs hourly, and the feet
every second.

It was a time and place where "everybody was a nothing."
And was paid what seems nothing to us now. Around 1900, for
a sixty-hour week pressers would make $500 a year, skilled
men $600 or $700, and cutters, the aristocrats of the trade,
$900. Women of course got less. Many worked 108 hours
weekly and got $3 to $6 for it. In a study of New York living
standards at that time, the Russell Sage Foundation concluded
$800 a year was the minimum for a decent life. Which meant
families had to take in boarders or put wife and children to
work to make ends meet.

By 1900, about 200,000 Jewish immigrants and their families
were in the garment trade. The greater part of the work was
no longer done through contractors, but by a host of small
manufacturers. For the worker, however, it was the same
thing—he still suffered from the old abuses of long hours, low
pay, and terrible conditions.

Few really wealthy Jews emerged among the eastern Europeans. Not many who became garment manufacturers got
rich quick. It was a tooth-and-nail competition and the man
who clawed his way up today could be kicked down tomorrow.

When the eastern European Jews began to work in the
garment trades in the early 1880s, labor had virtually no
rights. And public opinion couldn't care less about the working class. Most manufacturers paid no attention to the way
their workers lived. By 1890, 10 per cent of the population of
the big cities were living in slums as bad as any in Europe.
In New York, Chicago, Philadelphia, 90 per cent or more of
the slum population were of foreign birth or parentage. In
these "wildernesses of neglect" the Jewish immigrant, like

others, learned about an America different from that in the
dreams he came with. It was a Goldeneh Medina—but for only
1 per cent of the population. That 1 per cent enjoyed wealth
greater than the total of the remaining 99 per cent. "Never
before or since in American history have the rich been so rich
or the poor so poor," one historian has said.

What trade unions there were received no protection in law.
With unions so weak, wages, hours, and working conditions
were fixed by custom and the market. The flood of immigrants
made cheap labor plentiful, and the unions' position all the
weaker.

The Knights of Labor, formed after the Civil War, called
for an eight-hour day, for an end to child labor, for health
and safety laws, and for equal pay for equal work. Their
slogan was AN INJURY TO ONE IS AN INJURY TO ALL. Thousands
joined their ranks.

A rival national movement was started in 1886 by two Jews,
Samuel Gompers and Adolph Strasser of the Cigar Makers'
Union. The goal of the American Federation of Labor was
A FAIR DAY'S WAGE FOR A FAIR DAY'S WORK, and its method, to
form organizations for each of the skilled crafts. Gompers was
a heavy-set man, with a thick mop of hair and rimless glasses.
He had come over from England young and poor to find work
on the Lower East Side in the cigar-making shops. By 1890
he had made the AF of L the central force in American labor.
He got results for the limited group of skilled workers he tried
to reach. But what about the garment workers, this mass of
unorganized immigrants? Here in America the labor unions
either barred the foreign-born from joining or did nothing to
organize them. Unskilled and uneducated workers could find
no way to help themselves, to make their voices heard, their
needs felt. The east European Jews had been individuals in
the shtetl. To work together to improve their lives was something they had never tried. They came to America each with
his private dream of success. Taking a job in a shop would
be only a steppingstone to something better. They were ready
to starve themselves in a sweatshop to save a little money for

the day when they could raise themselves out of the ranks. Then too, the ties that bound people from the same shtetl or town hampered unionism. Contractors would lend passage money and give jobs to relatives or fellow townsmen—landsleit—and how could you be disloyal to them? Paternalism didn't lessen exploitation, but it made organization harder.

Unions did get started at last. Led by the United Hebrew Trades, they slowly made their way among the first-generation immigrants. The year 1890 was a turning point. The cloakmakers, led by young Joseph Barondess, won a strike, and union membership soared. Four unions were able to strike root in the trades dominated by Jews. First came the International Ladies' Garment Workers' Union, then the Cap Makers, the Fur Workers, and finally the Amalgamated Clothing Workers. It took several sensational events to win public support for the plight of the workers. The 1901 strike of waist and dress makers, led by the ILGWU, became known as "the uprising of the 20,000." In 1910 came a great general strike of 60,000 garment workers who shut down the whole industry. So bitter and bloody was the clash between bosses and workers (both Jewish) that the Jewish community stepped in to make peace. The lawyer Louis Brandeis, known as "the people's attorney," became the chief arbitrator. A "protocol of peace" was worked out which ended the biggest strike in the city's history by ending sweatshop conditions. Shorter hours, higher wages, improved working conditions were set; piecework labor in shop or home was eliminated, health standards were to be improved, and a permanent arbitration board was made up of labor, management, and public representatives. This principle of collective bargaining to settle future disputes was now accepted by all parties. It was a milestone in American labor history.

Six months later, in March 1911, a mass tragedy brought the garment workers again into the public spotlight. A fire broke out in the non-union Triangle Waist factory, trapping 850 workers, mostly young girls, behind illegally locked doors on the upper floors. The New York *World* described what happened:

> Before smoke or flame gave signs from the windows, the loss of life was fully under way. The first signs that people in the street knew that these three top stories had turned into red furnaces in which human creatures were being caught and incinerated was when screaming men and women and boys and girls crowded out on the many window ledges and threw themselves into the streets far below. They jumped with their clothing ablaze. The hair of some of the girls streamed up aflame as they leaped. Thud after thud sounded on the pavements. It is a ghastly fact that on both the Greene Street and Washington Place sides of the building there grew mounds of the dead and dying. And the worst horror of all was that in this heap of the dead now and then there stirred a limb or sounded a moan.
>
> Within the three flaming floors it was as frightful. There flames enveloped many so that they died instantly. When Fire Chief Croker could make his way into these three floors, he found sights that utterly staggered him, that sent him, a man used to viewing horrors, back and down into the street with quivering lips. The floors were black with smoke. And then he saw as the smoke drifted away bodies burned to bare bones. There were skeletons bending over sewing machines.

In ten minutes the holocaust killed 146, and crippled or disfigured many others. Fifty thousand silent marchers followed the charred victims to a common burial in the Workmen's Circle Cemetery. "The life of the lowliest worker," said Rabbi Stephen Wise, "is sacred and inviolable." No longer able to brush off such disasters as unpreventable "accidents,"

the state was forced to investigate labor conditions. Out of
the findings came new laws to protect the worker and make
his life more human. The Jews, New York's largest immigrant
group, had become "not only workmen with rights, but citizens
without shame."

Chapter 7

BREAD, HERRING, AND STEEL

"It is enough that I am a merchant," the peddler was saying to the New York *Tribune*'s reporter. "What is such a life? What can I do for my people or myself? My boy shall be a lawyer, learned and respected of men. And it is for that I stand here, sometimes when my feet ache so that I would gladly go and rest. My boy shall have knowledge. He shall go to college."

As soon as they arrived, east European Jews showed a burning thirst for knowledge. Luckily they came to a city where schooling from the first grade through college was free. The Jewish tradition prepared the immigrants to seize the opportunity for education. The more learning you had, the more life. The ignorant man had no one's respect. True, a father hoped too that his children would make a better living than he had. But this was only part of the goal. Not everyone succeeded. Some became doctors and some thieves. Some ended as professors and some as prostitutes.

For the Jews, as for all other immigrants, the schools were like an assembly line producing "Americans." Harry Golden came as a child from a Galician village in 1905. Four years later, he was "king" of his class, proudly marching beside his "queen" in a pageant of American history. He recalled that "When a new greenhorn came to the class, frightened and confused, unable to manage any English, all knew that within six months he would be able to stand before us and, heavy accent and all, recite:

> I love the name of Washington,
> I love my country, too.
> I love the flag, the dear old flag,
> The red, the white, the blue."

In Golden's class when he graduated from P.S. 20 were the sons of immigrants, like himself, who would make their mark in the world: the composer George Gershwin, the actors Paul Muni and Edward G. Robinson, and Senator Jacob Javits. So the schools made citizens out of the immigrants. And did it within a single generation. At a cost, however. Not in money, but in something more valuable. The children were stripped of their Old World heritage. Their teachers—different in origin and often in religion—made them ashamed of the language their parents spoke, and of their people's ancient tradition. What they were as eastern European Jews with a distinct past —their ethnic identity—was ignored. It was not "American," so it had no value. These "dirty, ignorant foreigners" had to be trained to be blindly loyal to the flag and the government of the United States.

The school competed with the home for the children's loyalty. The father had been the authority. Now there was a rival, the teacher. The gap between parents and children widened. As the children grew older, they felt forced to choose between their parents' ways and the "American" way. Some settled for a kind of in-between life. At home they did what was expected of them; outside, they were a part of the life of the street or the school. America taught them the goal was to get ahead, to make good, to be a success. If their fathers had not made it, it was easy to believe something was wrong with them.

The schools did not recognize the fact that all Americans have roots in two cultures. One is their own immigrant background and heritage. The other is the American, which has meant an Anglo-Saxon culture tainted by racism. Most of the schools did not seek out and encourage the use of the rich treasure house of what is diverse and different among us. Instead, they ground the immigrants down into the lowest common denominator.

What happened to Yiddish—the mama-loshen (the mother tongue)—is an example. Yiddish is an old language, written in the Hebrew alphabet and using many Hebrew words. Most of its words, however, come from Loez, a mixture of Old French and Old Italian, and from the German spoken in the Middle Ages. But as the Jews wandered across Europe, the language picked up words from Russia, Poland, Latvia, Lithuania, Galicia, Bessarabia, Hungary, Romania. Then the Jews reached America, and English sifted into the language. When you translate Yiddish into English, you spell it any way you want to, as it sounds in your own ear. It is full of variations, a tongue of many tongues to be spoken with gusto. It can be funny and it can be savage. It can make you cry, or laugh, or both at once.

Writers in the old country—Mendele Mocher Sephorim, Isaac Leib Peretz, Sholem Aleichem—were the classical masters of Yiddish. But here the language had suffered neglect by the earlier German immigrants. Many of the Jewish intellectuals of the 1880s didn't like Yiddish either. They looked down on it as the language of the country folk of the shtetl. They preferred their Russian or German. It was the new Yiddish press, and especially Abraham Cahan, founder and editor of the *Jewish Daily Forward,* who midwifed the rebirth of Yiddish.

The popular press taught vast numbers of Jews American values in Yiddish. And Cahan insisted it be in the simplest Yiddish, the language by which the workers of the old East Side lived. Cahan himself wrote, said one of his readers, in a language "grafted out of bread, herring, and steel." For generations the *Forward* served American Jews as friend, teacher, and guide. Daily it advised its readers on how to survive in America. Cahan fought for labor's rights, for democratic socialism, for good literature and theater. He published the work of statesmen, revolutionaries, philosophers, poets—all in Yiddish. His columns were packed with news and features. His best-loved innovation was *Das Bintel Brief*—"A Bundle of Letters." Jews poured out their troubles and asked for advice ("Esteemed Editor: My son is already twenty-six years old and doesn't want to get married. He says he is a Socialist and he is too busy. Socialism is socialism but getting married is important, too.") In the pages of the Yiddish press you can find the soul of those immigrant generations.

Yiddish remained the language of that first generation of immigrants, but the editors knew that sooner or later their readers would move on to the English press. That was the measure of becoming American. Like the children of all other immigrant groups, the Jews were turned away from their fathers' native tongue.

Even more than their press did the Jewish immigrants love their Yiddish theater. On the stage were real people like themselves, playing a life that moved the audiences now to wrenching sobs and now to hysterical laughter. It was a new theater, begun in Romania only in the 1870s. Its first playwright was Abraham Goldfaden. One of his most popular pieces was *The Recruits*, a farce about two Jews drafted into military service who get into so many scrapes the Army gladly throws them out. Within ten years his plays and those of many others were being produced on the Lower East Side. There were romantic musicals to see, historical operas, folk comedies, "greenhorn" melodramas of immigrant life, topical plays about strikes and floods and murders and pogroms, and Yiddish adaptations of world classics. The audiences were so passionately fond of theater a family would spend half its small earnings to come see the plays and meet their friends, to gossip, eat, laugh, cry, adore the actors.

For the East Sider, the public library was a great magnet. As soon as school closed at three, the children would rush to the Chatham Square branch to draw out books in English at the rate of a thousand a day. An *Evening Post* reporter, watching them, wrote that "The Jewish child has more than an

The Yiddish theater was an important part of the
Jewish culture. Sometimes a family would spend half
their earnings to come to see the plays and meet and
talk with their friends.

eagerness for mental food; it is an intellectual mania. He wants to learn everything in the library and everything the librarians know. He is interested not only in knowledge that will be of practical benefit, but in knowledge for its own sake."

The adults had not only the library but free evening schools and free lectures. Crowds overflowed the Great Hall at Cooper Union to hear speakers on history, literature, ethics, religion, labor, the race problem. Debates on socialism were the most popular. Lecturers called the audiences "the most thoroughly alive" they ever talked to.

After having been pent up for centuries in the Old World, Jewish energy was exploding in every direction. Maurice Hindus, a Russian immigrant, said no place was so tempestuously alive with movements and ideals as the heart of the Lower East Side. Dozens of groups of every political belief blossomed, each passionately resolved to save something or somebody. In the cafes and on the street they argued furiously with one another, each claiming the true gospel of hope and deliverance. To the young immigrant it was a wildly exciting world. It made him ask a million questions he never thought of before. Life was stretched beyond the bounds of street, school, or shop.

The sweatshop was not for young Hindus. He turned to farming for a time. Later, he became a reporter and the author of many useful books. There were others like him—a minority of the immigrants—who did not want to be either shopworkers or businessmen. In America they had a chance to satisfy the ambition to become a professional. With the Jewish respect for learning, they studied hard at night while by day they worked in a store or factory. They became physicians, dentists, pharmacists, scientists, lawyers. They found careers in the theater, publishing, journalism, government, teaching. Occupations closed to Jews in the Old World gradually opened to them in the New.

The cost of "making good" often proved high, whether in business or the professions. Competition was frantic. The pace was blistering. Fear of failure was ever present. If you ran hard enough and thought only of yourself you might make it. But what might happen to a man's integrity, his ideals, his humanity?

Chapter 8

SELF-HELP AND SOCIAL JUSTICE

"Will the Russian or Romanian Jew, now an object of pity owing to his defective education, his lack of culture, his pauperism, his utter helplessness, drag American Judaism down from the honorable position it has attained?"

It was the year 1889 when Rabbi Kaufmann Kohler voiced this worry. He was one of the most eminent German Jews in America. He spoke for his solidly established brethren. They looked upon the east European immigrants as raw and uncivilized, and at first would have nothing to do with them. These "outlandish foreigners" would stir up anti-Semitism, they feared.

But as the tide of immigration rose, the German Jews realized that no matter what they felt, non-Jews would identify them with the newcomers. So they had better help to Americanize the east Europeans swiftly. Ever since the Diaspora, mutual aid had been the key to Jewish survival. Tzedakeh—righteousness and charity—was a Hebrew ideal. And the mitzvah too—the doing of a good deed. It was natural, then, to start organizations to help the newcomers with money, guidance, training, education. The United Hebrew Charities provided food, lodging, medical services, jobs. In 1884 the Hebrew Sheltering and Immigrant Aid Society was formed. In 1893 the National Council of Jewish Women was founded to protect the rights of immigrant women. The Industrial Removal Office steered thousands of immigrants past New York and into smaller cities around the country. The Baron de Hirsch Fund helped move Jews into light industry and agriculture.

But the immigrants helped themselves, too. Almost every household had pushkes. They were small tin boxes, with slots for pennies and nickels, charity boxes a little old man with a black bag would come around every week to empty. That was personal giving. The immigrants formed into groups to provide mutual benefits. Many were fraternal societies—landsmanschaft —made up of Jews who came from the same village or area in Europe. (It was a tradition going back to the sixth century B.C.E., when the Judean exiles in Babylonia organized themselves by their Palestinian town of origin.) The main purpose was to help one another. They did it through medical, unemployment, and strike insurance, interest-free loans, sick benefits and disability payments, funeral costs and burial plots.

The landsmanschaft began to replace the religious societies in providing these benefits. By 1914, New York alone counted more than five hundred of them, touching the lives of almost every immigrant home. They founded their own hospitals (Beth Israel, in 1889, was the first of many) and their own homes to care for the aged and the orphaned. They started travelers-aid societies, and societies to help widows, children, prisoners, unwed mothers, the deaf, the blind, the crippled.

Young Men's and Young Women's Hebrew Associations developed into community centers for education and recreation. Social-service agencies, such as the Henry Street Settlement in New York or Hull House in Chicago, were launched by social reformers to prepare young and old for life in America. The aim of their staff was "to work *with* the people, rather than to work for the people. Not for ourselves, but for others" was their motto.

Seven-year-old Harry Roskolenko went to the Educational Alliance settlement "to study small nails, little hammers, short saws—to become a carpenter. I would remake our Russian-Jewish home with American bookcases for my ten self-owned books, found in a native garbage can; with a stool, to sit much closer to the big Russian stove; a chinning bar, to make more muscle and frighten some Irish; a towel rack for my private towel—and little things that would mean big things to me, still wondering then whether I would ever become four feet high."

At the settlement's classes, which ran day and night the year round, the boys and girls learned all about birds, flowers, tides, rocks. There were departments for girls in homemaking and for young mothers in child rearing. There was music for fiddlers and hornblowers and quartets. There were reading rooms for men and study halls for children. There were classes in Hebrew, Yiddish, Russian, English, classes in the Torah and classes in Greek philosophy, lessons in staging Shakespeare and playing basketball. Through the art department went such students as Ben Shahn, Peter Blume, Jo Davidson, Leonard Baskin, Adolph Gottlieb, Jacob Epstein. Out of the settlement houses came boys who made good, like the tycoon David Sarnoff. And boys who would not adapt, and became gangsters, like Meyer Lansky.

Soon it seemed sensible to pull together all these efforts. The Federation of Jewish Philanthropies was started and spread everywhere. In 1906, wealthy German Jews founded the American Jewish Committee to defend Jewish interests. The United Jewish Appeal's purpose was to raise money for Jewish causes at home and abroad. At the beginning of the First World War the Joint Distribution Committee merged some existing agencies to carry on relief work in Europe. At the war's end, the American Jewish Congress was formed. One goal was to work to establish a Jewish national home in Palestine. Another was to win legal recognition of the civil rights and liberties of Jews everywhere in the world.

If some said that money donated for philanthropy was conscience money, still it was the Judaic thing to do. Under the biblical tradition such giving did not rob the receiver of his dignity. Was not every Jew responsible for his fellow Jew? And for the stranger at the gate?

The religious east Europeans hoped to provide a genuine Jewish education for their sons in America. That meant

schooling in the Torah and the Talmud. In the old country it
was done through full-time day schools. Attempts to do the
same thing here came to little. Because the newcomers were
bent on Americanization, the free public schools came first.
Almost all their children were enrolled in them. But only a
fourth got any religious instruction in the time left over, on
afternoons or Sundays.

Children three to ten went to a cheder and later to the
Talmud Torah for three hours every afternoon. Most of the
pupils were boys. There were cheders of all kinds—Sephardic,
Levantine, Ashkenazi. The rebbe (teacher) was usually an
old man dressed all in black, from his round broad-brimmed
hat to his long, rusty coat, whose pockets were stuffed with old
letters from Europe, tattered books, and Yiddish papers. "You
learned, or you were slapped," Harry Roskolenko recalls. That
had been the method in all the ghettos of eastern Europe. "You
learned what you wanted to learn, by rote, under stress, while
asleep, while rushing to the toilet, while rushing back" to the
little table or desk and the hard bench.

But soon it did not seem to matter. What use was the
cheder in preparing a child for this new life? In eastern
Europe, religion was vital to the Jew confined to the ghetto or
the shtetl. In American society religion played no central role.
Even the children who had the best Talmud Torah education
were as likely to drop away from orthodoxy as those who had
none.

The synagogues had multiplied rapidly as the east European
immigration swelled. In 1880 there were 270 in New York. By
1916 the number was 1900. Most of the congregations were
small. Any ten Jews were free to form a synagogue and worship
as they willed. Landsleit tended to gather in their own tiny
synagogues—converted stores or tenement flats where you could
meet old friends and renew yourself in worship. The newcomers were deeply attached to the religion that had governed
their lives. But much less so their children. Nor was the first
American-born generation interested in Yiddish culture. The
Yiddish press tried, but failed, to capture them by printing

English-language sections. Grandma and Grandpa might read the *Forward* in the evening, but the children didn't want to.

Even before leaving eastern Europe, some Jews had given up both the traditional religion and Yiddish. New ideas from the West had reached them, especially those who had moved from the small towns to the cities. Socialism appealed to many as a way out of oppression. It would cure anti-Semitism as well as solve economic problems, they believed. Others looked to setting up a Jewish state in Palestine as the answer. Some simply wished to assimilate.

The masses of Jews in eastern Europe had been allowed no part in government. The state was the tool of royalty, of the rich, of the gentry. Their interests were against the poor. They used their power to pile taxes higher, to conscript young men, to whip up pogroms. They lived off the sweat of the people.

Here in America the immigrants found they had a right to become citizens. And they soon learned the advantages. To get a job, to get a license, to open a business, to do a hundred and one ordinary things meant having dealings with some official or other. And a little oil would make the machinery work better. Favors were always being asked in a society which had become increasingly corrupt after the Civil War. And needed even more if one broke a law, by intent or by mistake. It helped to have friends in the right places. The politician could pull a string, open a door, obtain a hearing. And he expected a vote in return for a favor. If he didn't get it, he had painful ways of showing his displeasure.

The bosses of the city political machines used the immigrants to maintain themselves in power. Voters were openly bribed just outside the polls. Naïve immigrants were taught to sell their ballot for a dollar or two. But gradually the newcomers came to realize that control of government should mean more than the handing out of favors. Why shouldn't state power be used to advance freedom and improve the general welfare? By the 1890s, millions of Americans were asking such questions. Henry George's book *Progress and Poverty*, a passionate portrait of hard times, had won an enormous audience. The book made them concerned about inequality in American life. Then Edward Bellamy's best-seller novel, *Looking Backward*, showed them what life could be like if the social, economic, and political system was organized to eliminate poverty, disease, and corruption.

Many began to think the government should be an educational and ethical agency to help make life better for everyone. Why shouldn't labor be treated fairly, people began to ask. Wages and working conditions ought to be decent and prices just. Churchmen began to preach the "social gospel." After visiting New York's slums one Protestant minister wrote he had seen that "man is treated as a thing to produce more things. Men are hired as hands and not as men. They are paid only enough to maintain their working capacity and not enough to develop their manhood. When their working force is exhausted, they are flung aside without consideration of their human needs. Jesus asked, 'Is not a man more than a sheep?' Our industry says 'No.'"

In the 1890s the new Populist Party elected many of its partisans to office and nearly won the presidency. Its bold call for action to curb organized wealth and equalize opportunity was debated everywhere. A new period of American life opened, the Progressive Era. Journalists played a great role in the awakening. Men and women investigated what was wrong with American society and published their findings in magazines of mass circulation. The great reporter Jacob Riis went down to the Lower East Side with pen and camera and came out with an indictment of immigrant slum life called *How the Other Half Lives*. The photographer Lewis Hine did the same, exposing the horrors of child labor. Both showed that public neglect was as responsible as private greed for fostering slum and sweatshop.

The muckraking journalists opened people's eyes to where their country was going. They stirred conscience and started people thinking about what had to be done to make freedom and equality something real, not just slogans.

In the face of great injustice, some thought reform wasn't

enough. They wanted radical change. Among them were the Jewish intellectuals who came from Russia in the 1880s. They felt they were entering a new era. In America they expected to realize their ideals. They tried to build agricultural communes in Louisiana and Oregon, and when they failed, came back to the Lower East Side. Here they experimented with tenement communes, co-operative laundries, and vegetarian diets. They went into radical politics and helped organize Jewish unions. At last Jews were quitting the old humiliating occupations and straightening their ghetto-bent backs. "Neither wealthier nor more pious but more of a man" was the goal they held out to their brothers.

New York had become the center of the Socialist movement. Its rank and file were immigrants, mostly the Jewish needle trade workers. "To this hard-working people," wrote the historian David A. Shannon, "Socialism was more than just a political movement; it was a way of life. In some neighborhoods one grew up to be a Socialist, a reader of Abraham Cahan's *Jewish Daily Forward*, in Yiddish, or the *Call*, in English, and a member of one of the needle trade unions just as naturally as in some other parts of the country one grew up to be a Republican and a reader of the *Saturday Evening Post*."

Jews entered the radical movement because it reflected their concern for social justice, which is basic to Judaism. The radical parties were the parties of movement, of change. It was natural that Jews should tend to join such parties in their unending search for true freedom and the equality, especially the east Europeans, who had been persecuted so badly in the old country. Numbers had joined the Russian revolutionary movement. In 1897 they had formed the Jewish Workers Federation (Yiddishe Arbeiter Bund). It spread Socialist ideas in Yiddish among the growing Jewish working class. Tsar Nicholas II, dreading a revolution, followed the old custom of blaming all his country's troubles on the Jews. In 1903 his police chief, Count Plehve, stage-directed the Kishinev pogrom. He launched rumors of a ritual murder by the Jews, which led unthinking mobs to carry out a terrible massacre. By setting one part of the population against another, the authorities hoped to relieve the pressure for constitutional reform. The bloody circus was meant, too, as a warning for the Jews to stay out of the revolutionary movement.

Pogroms (the Russian word *pogromit* means "to destroy") are mentioned in the history books, but what one was really like is seldom described. Immigrant parents, asked about such experiences, usually refused to give any details. A Jewish nurse working in the Jewish Hospital of Odessa has set down what happened when the telephone rang one day and someone cried, "The Moldvanko [Jewish slum quarter] is running in blood; send nurses and doctors!"

Together the staffs of the Jewish Hospital and the City Hospital rushed to the scene of the pogrom. The non-Jewish physicians hung silver crosses about the necks of the Jews so that hooligans would not harm them. When they reached the Moldvanko, wrote the nurse,

> We could not see, for the feathers were flying like snow. The blood was already up to our ankles on the pavement and in the yards. The uproar was deafening but we could hear the hooligans' fierce cries of "Hooray! Kill the Jews!" on all sides. It was enough to hear such words. They could turn your hair grey, but we went on. We had no time to think. All our thoughts were to pick up wounded ones, and to try to rescue some uninjured who were in hiding. We put bandages on them to make it appear they were wounded. We put them in the ambulance and carried them to the hospital, too. So at the Jewish Hospital we had five thousand injured and seven thousand uninjured to feed and protect for two weeks. Some were left without homes, without clothes, and children were even without parents.
>
> The procession of the pogrom was led by about ten Catholic [Greek] Sisters with about forty or fifty of their schoolchildren. They carried ikons or pictures of

Jesus and sang "God save the Tsar." They were followed by a crowd containing hundreds of men and women murderers yelling "Bey Zhida!" which means "Kill the Jews!" With these words they ran into the yards where there were fifty or a hundred tenants. They rushed in like tigers. Soon they began to throw children out of the windows of the second, third, or fourth stories. They would take a poor, innocent six-months-old baby, who could not possibly have done any harm in this world, and throw it down to the pavement. You can imagine it could not live after it struck the ground, but this did not satisfy the stony-hearted murderers. They then rushed up to the child, seized it and broke its little arm and leg bones into three or four pieces, then wrung its neck too. They laughed and yelled, so carried away with pleasure at their successful work . . .

It was not enough for them to open up a woman's abdomen and take out the child which she carried, but they took time to stuff the abdomen with straw and fill it up . . . It was not enough for them to cut out an old man's tongue and cut off his nose, but they drove nails into the eyes also. You wonder how they had enough time to carry away everything of value —money, gold, silver, jewels—and still be able to do so much fancy killing, but oh, my friends, all the time for three days and three nights was theirs . . .

I remember what happened to my own class-mates. They were two who came from a small town to Odessa to become midwives. These girls ran to the school to hide themselves as it was a government school, and they knew the hooligans would not dare to come in there. But the dean of the school had ordered they should not be admitted, because they were Jewish, as if they had different blood running in their veins. So when they came, the watchman refused to open the doors, according to his instructions. The crowd

In Russia during the early 1900s the chief of police
directed the Kishinev pogrom, which set the different

section of the population against one another. The
pogroms resulted in the murder of thousands of Jews.

of hooligans found them outside the doors of the hospital. They abused them right there in the middle of the street . . .

Some will ask, where were the soldiers and the police? They were sent to protect, but on arriving, joined in with the murderers. However, the police put disguises on over their uniforms. Later, when they were brought to the hospital with other wounded, we found their uniforms underneath their disguises . . .

More and more Jews fled the Tsar's crumbling empire. Among them were revolutionaries who preferred exile to a Tsarist prison. In 1906, 152,000 entered the United States, and the next year, 148,000, the peak period of Jewish immigration. Now there were about a million Jews in Greater New York. It was the largest Jewish population of any city in the world. Big enough to make politicians of all parties contend for their support. By 1900 the Lower East Side was able to elect its first Jewish congressman, a Democrat, Henry Goldfogle.

Goldfogle's seat was eventually taken by the Lower East Side's beloved labor lawyer, Meyer London. He was the first Socialist to win any office in New York. He was also the first congressman of Russian birth. "Perhaps the sun will shine on the East Side from now on!" cried out one jubilant voter when the news of London's election came in. That night thousands of East Siders went out to sing and dance in the streets. They greeted Meyer London's victory as twin to their successful battle for trade union rights.

Even candidates for the presidency began to take into account the needs of Jewish voters. President Theodore Roosevelt appointed Oscar Straus to be his Secretary of Commerce and Labor. Straus had headed the National Committee for the Relief of Sufferers by Russian Massacres. But even as the pogroms multiplied in Russia, American sentiment against immigration was increasing. Jews wanted desperately to keep America's door open to victims of persecution. But powerful forces were trying to slam it shut.

Chapter 9

"ONLY GENTILES NEED APPLY"

All these newcomers to the United States—did they really belong?

It was a question some Americans had begun asking by the 1880s. Earlier, not many worried about it. For more than a century American immigration policy had been an open door to all who wished to enter. True, there had always been some who feared "foreigners." (John Winthrop of colonial Massachusetts didn't like the Scotch-Irish and Benjamin Franklin detested the Germans.) But what else was America but a nation of nations? English, Africans, Scotch-Irish, Welsh, Germans, Swedes, Irish, Danes, Finns—all had come before the Revolution. The new nation's first great wave of immigration came in the early 1800s. It landed a quarter-million Irish on these shores. People with anti-foreign feelings pictured them as agents of the Pope sent to subvert America. The Know-Nothings, a political party of "native" Americans, sprang up in the 1850s to keep foreigners and especially Catholics from public office and to make naturalization more difficult.

The Chinese were the next target of the nativists. By 1880 there were 75,000 Chinese on the West Coast, working as railroad laborers, miners, laundrymen, cigar makers, house servants. White workers, who feared cheap Chinese labor would undermine their wages and conditions, campaigned to rid the country of them. In 1882 the U. S. Congress passed the Chinese

Exclusion Act suspending immigration of all Chinese laborers for ten years and forbidding the naturalization of Chinese.

A second wave of immigration made up mostly of Germans, Scandinavians, and English hit its peak in this same year. Just as it subsided, a third great wave began gathering force. Now it was no longer the north Europeans, but people of southern and eastern Europe who wanted to come in. As their numbers shot up toward the turn of the century, many Americans became alarmed. They asked for laws to keep out these Russians, Slavs, Poles, Italians, Greeks, Jews.

This Congress was not ready to do. A few months after putting up bars to the Chinese, it simply barred criminals, paupers, and the insane, and required all immigrants to prove they would not become a public charge. If they couldn't support themselves, they had to show a document from a friend or relative pledging support.

What did the older Americans have against the newcomers? First, they blamed them for their poverty. They looked at life in the slums and said it was the immigrants' fault that there was dirt and crime and ignorance and hunger. The truth was, if the newcomers had been able to find jobs at decent wages, these conditions would not have existed.

And then the immigrants were accused of sticking together, of living clannishly in their own groups and not mixing with outsiders. It was only natural that the Jews, for instance, should want to live among their own people. And where else could they afford to live but in the East Side slums? When they did earn enough to move outside the ghetto, the "true Americans" were not inclined to welcome them to their neighborhoods.

The earlier arrivals had come to hold the view that American civilization was really Anglo-Saxon or Nordic at root. Only the people who had come to the New World before the great migrations were the "true Americans." (Not including Indians or blacks, of course.) If these strange breeds of new immigrants wanted to be Americanized, they must shape their life in this Anglo-Saxon mold.

So they said—but they really didn't believe the strangers could or should be assimilated. They trotted out the "evidence" of American scientists who claimed that man was divided into inferior and superior races. The higher Nordic stocks from which they said the Founding Fathers came would be overwhelmed by the lower breeds from eastern and southern Europe—unless immigration were restricted. Such ideas were the forerunners of Nazi racial doctrine.

By this time prejudice against the latecomers had become a habit. Every experience the "true American" had with an individual Italian, Irishman, Pole, or Jew—with any outsider— became the basis for a stereotype. Italians were murderers, Irish drunks, Poles stupid, and Jews shysters. Anything or anybody differing from himself was to the Anglo-Saxon foreign and inferior.

It was at this time that the word "anti-Semitism" came into use. A writer in Germany coined it in 1879 when he proposed that the rights of all Jews be taken away. A "Semite" is a person who speaks a language of one of the peoples called Semitic, who originally lived in the Middle East. The best-known such languages are Arabic and Hebrew. In Europe the only people who spoke a Semitic language were the Jews. So the word "Semite" came to mean a Jew. And anti-Semitism now refers to actions or beliefs designed to be harmful to Jews as a group, or to any individual because he is a Jew.

After the Civil War, anti-Semitism found expression in many forms. Fire insurance companies, for instance, refused to issue policies covering Jewish merchants. A New York company of the National Guard barred all Jews from membership. Tony Pastor's cabaret staged an anti-Semitic burlesque called "Jew Trouble at Manhattan Beach." The New York *Times* published a piece calling the Lower East Side "the eyesore of New York and perhaps the filthiest place on the western continent . . . impossible for a Christian to live there." The Jews "cannot be lifted up to a higher plane," the writer said, "because they do not want to be."

Even those Jews who had already lifted themselves up to

"a higher plane" found out anti-Semites were no readier to accept "better-class" Jews. The event which offered dramatic proof occurred at Saratoga. Each summer the cream of American society vacationed at the famous resort. One day in 1877 the Grand Union, the world's largest hotel, turned away Joseph Seligman and his party, declaring it would no longer admit Jews. Seligman, one of America's leading bankers and a power in the Republican Party, wrote a fighting letter to the hotel's owner which made the issue of anti-Semitism front-page news.

Jews had been kept out of other places before—but quietly. Now hotels and clubs in the Adirondacks boldly advertised "Hebrews need not apply." And other institutions followed suit. The New York Bar Association blackballed Jews. The Union League Club of New York shut them out. At City College the fraternities barred Jewish students. Anti-Semitism had come out in the open. Some Americans, proud of a heritage of freedom and equality, protested anti-Semitism. But far more accepted the racist justification for discrimination, and went along with it.

The pattern of discrimination began to spread. Soon a quota system was adopted by colleges all over the country limiting the number of Jews they would admit. The Help Wanted columns began to state "Only Gentiles need apply." Barriers were put up to the entry of Jews in many professions and in some unions. Jews could not buy or build homes in certain neighborhoods, even in whole towns. Their children could not get into private schools.

How anti-Semitism affected workers on the job is told in a letter to the press from an eighteen-year-old machinist:

> It is common knowledge that my trade is run mainly by the Gentiles and, working among the Gentiles, I have seen things that cast a dark shadow on the American labor scene.
>
> I worked in a shop in a small town in New Jersey, with twenty Gentiles. There was one other Jew besides me, and both of us endured the greatest hardships.

That we were insulted goes without saying. At times
we were even beaten up. We work in an area where
there are many factories, and once, when we were
leaving the shop, a group of workers fell on us like
hoodlums and beat us. To top it off, we and one of
our attackers were arrested. The hoodlum was let out
on bail, but we, beaten and bleeding, had to stay in
jail. At the trial, they fined the hoodlum eight dollars
and let him go free.

After that I went to work on a job in Brooklyn. As
soon as they found out I was a Jew they began to
torment me so that I had to leave the place. I have
already worked at many places, and I either have to
leave, voluntarily, or they fire me because I am a
Jew . . .

Hearts hardened to the point where *Century* magazine
could run an article defending the pogroms breaking out all
over Russia. Its attack upon the Jews was so vicious the poet
Emma Lazarus insisted upon answering it in the next issue.

Frank P. Sargent, the U. S. Commissioner General of Immigration, told a reporter that "the time has come when every
American citizen who is ambitious for the national future must
regard with grave misgiving the mighty tide of immigration
that, unless something is done, will soon poison or at least
pollute the very fountainhead of American life and progress."

That distrust of the stranger and fear of the future he might
shape triggered powerful feelings. Especially in time of
trouble. In the 1890s a major depression created millions of
victims of unemployment and hunger. Demagogues said the
Jews were to blame. Preachers and politicians fired up audiences with dire warnings that "the time is coming when the
Jews will rule the world. They are already its financial masters.
In a few years they will control every profession and every
branch of commerce and industry."

Rulers? Masters? Some of the German Jews had built large
fortunes during a period of headlong economic growth. Their

banking firms played a role in America's rapid development after the Civil War. But they were mostly engaged in financing light industry and retail trade. They were never great financial powers like such non-Jews as Morgan, Mellon, Rockefeller, Gould, Harriman, Astor, Du Pont. To charge the Jews with running the country was ridiculous.

Facts and logic mean little, however, in the face of irrational fears and hatreds. So whether he lived in a Fifth Avenue mansion or an East Side slum, whether he was a banker or a sweatshop worker, the Jew was painted as a menace to America. He was "foreign," "mysterious," "threatening." Jews as they really were, with their virtues and their faults, could not find room in the minds of a society burdened by religious and racial prejudices.

Learning that high society would not accept them, the German Jewish banking and business families developed their own exclusive social group. They married within the group and carried on a social life under its shelter. They lived on the scale of the rich, but avoided showing off their wealth. Their philanthropy was generous, and so were their contributions to the arts and to scholarship.

It was to fight discrimination that the American Jewish Committee was formed in 1906. Backing came from the wealthy German Jews. The goal was to protect the civil and religious rights of Jews and to meet any danger that threatened Jews abroad. At that moment it meant helping the eastern European Jews suffering from Russian pogroms, and at the same time fighting efforts to restrict immigration, which would have cut off their escape.

To counter anti-Semitism the Anti-Defamation League of B'nai B'rith was founded in 1913. Soon it was pioneering in interfaith understanding. Because a threat to the liberty or equality of one group is a threat to all, ADL worked to make the ideal of democracy a reality for all Americans, of whatever creed or color.

The effort to restrict immigration always rose in time of social crisis, such as the outbreak of the First World War in

1914. Patriotic fever inflamed the country. Everything foreign was under suspicion. Distrust of "outsiders" took a violent turn in Georgia in 1915. Leo Frank, a Jew from the North, was accused of murdering a girl and convicted on flimsy evidence. Tom Watson, a political leader who had long attacked the Catholics, now seized on the Jews as a target. The way to get rid of Jewish interference in Georgia was to execute Frank, he said. When the governor commuted Frank's sentence, Watson's inflamed followers took Frank from jail and lynched him.

Pressure was put on foreigners to become American quickly or go back where they came from. At last, in 1917, over the veto of President Wilson, Congress passed a bill providing for a literacy test that would bar adult immigrants unable to read. The expectation was that this would keep out most of the people from southern and eastern Europe.

Aliens were discriminated against in some fields of work and many aliens accused of being radical were deported in the Red Scare that seized America after the Russian Revolution of 1917. In both Europe and America, anti-Semites spread charges that the Jews had sparked the Revolution and now controlled it. Henry Ford, the world-famous auto magnate, spent millions on anti-Semitism. His weekly newspaper, the *Dearborn Independent*, with a national circulation of 700,000, collected old anti-Semitic libels about a Jewish plot to rule the world. For seven years Ford printed them in issue after issue, until a lawsuit forced him to make a public apology to all American Jews. (Years later the Nazis published the same articles.) The Ku Klux Klan, a secret society originally aimed against blacks, was revived. Now it was also against Catholics and Jews, against everybody not white, Anglo-Saxon, and Protestant. Its appeal to racism won it five million members in the early 1920s, chiefly in the South and Midwest.

When immigrants began coming in again after the war, the literacy test proved to be less of a barrier than its backers had hoped. Now they called for a quota system. Laws passed in 1921 were based upon ethnic quotas. They virtually excluded the people of eastern and southern Europe, and gave preference to the old Nordic groups. Total entry was set at about 150,000 a year. The door to America was no longer open to all. In 1924, the last year of mass immigration, 50,000 Jews entered the country. In the next year, 10,000. The tide of Jewish immigration had been dammed.

In 1927 Congress again revised the immigration laws. It kept the quota system, ended the total exclusion of Asians, and added provisions to keep out "subversives" and to permit deportation of Communists, whether citizens or not. From time to time after that Congress voted exceptions for refugee individuals or groups, such as Hungarians and Cubans.

In 1965 a new immigration act dropped the whole racist national-origins system of the 1920s. It set a quota of 170,000 immigrants per year, on a first-come, first-served policy, with no one country allowed more than 20,000.

But this is getting ahead of the story. Two things happened in the 1930s which changed life for everyone, and for the Jews had a special significance: the Great Depression, and the rise of Adolf Hitler.

Chapter 10

DEPRESSION—AND DESTRUCTION

For years "The First Deposit" was one of the most popular sketches performed on the Yiddish stage. It told of an immigrant who rushes to the bank with his first earned dollar. Panicky over what might happen to it, he stays away from his job and neglects eating and sleeping to keep an around-the-clock vigil at the bank. He guards its door at night so that no robbers will break in and during the day hangs around inside to see that the bankers don't dream up some crazy scheme to lose his money.

Suddenly the sketch stopped getting howls of laughter from the audience. On December 30, 1930, the Bank of the United States, whose headquarters were on Delancey Street, closed down. Most of its 400,000 depositors were Jews, a fifth of the city's Jewish population. They lost their life savings. Wiped out were the tiny holdings of widows, the money set aside to send children to college, to pay for medical emergencies, to buy partnerships, to open a store or a small business, to give a daughter a good wedding.

By the fall of 1932 over six thousand banks—about one fourth of the country's total—had closed their doors. Nine million people who believed their cash had been safely stored deep inside steel vaults never saw it again. The Depression had begun with the stock market crash of October 1929. Within two months several million people were out of work. Business

came to a dead halt. Salespeople were fired from the stores, factories cut down on production, work on new buildings stopped,
credit was strangled, business and industry ran out of funds. By
1933, there were about fourteen million unemployed. One
fourth of the nation—men, women, and children—belonged to
families with no regular income.

Thousands of Jewish businesses were among those that
went bankrupt. Doctors and dentists lost patients, storekeepers
lost customers, landlords lost rents, lawyers lost clients, workers (the garment industry was badly hit) lost jobs. Education
was crippled. Teachers were fired, pupils crowded together,
hours cut, classrooms closed.

Those who were well off before the crash were usually not
harmed by it. The old money, the great American fortunes
built in the nineteenth century, stood solid. That was true too
of the wealthy German Jewish families. But the east Europeans,
like the new rich generally, were often ruined.

It meant cutting down on the philanthropy that had sup-
ported many valuable charitable and educational institutions.
Still, a great number serving neighborhoods—orphanages, nurs-
eries, Hebrew schools, clinics—managed to stay open. Both
supporters and staff were too devoted to let them collapse in
the face of the great new need. The number of families getting
relief from Jewish welfare agencies increased by 40 to 100 per
cent in 1931. Out of pride, Jews in need were often slow to
apply for help. The landsmanschaften, which operated with no
publicity, did all they could to offer aid.

In the thirties the American Jewish community was still
made up largely of east European immigrants. They had produced few capitalists. The really rich were only a thin layer
atop the Jewish millions. Almost everyone had started in
poverty, and few of those who had made it were able to forget
what they had come from. There were no fixed class barriers in
the marginal world they shared. People shifted up or down, all
the while feeling more tied to their common immigrant roots
than divided by income differences.

In a sense, the Jewish economy was ghettoized. The garment

manufacturer and his workers were all Jews, and the clothes they made reached the country mostly through Jewish buyers and retailers. The Jewish doctor's patients, the Jewish lawyer's clients were Jews too, usually. And the trades and occupations that served them were also generally made up of Jews.

The situation was not peculiar to the Jews. Like the other immigrants, whether Irish or Italian, German or Swedish, they had settled where they found their own kind, where they could feel at home, use their own language, get work and help, marry their own people, keep their own style of living.

But concentrated as they were in New York and a few other eastern and midwestern cities, the Jews had not realized how isolated they were from non-Jews. Since the 1920s Jews had been moving about inside New York. They had gone from neighborhood to neighborhood, or borough to borough, spreading from Manhattan to the Bronx, Brooklyn, and Queens. Manhattan's Jewish population dropped steadily.

Still, until the Depression, few moved away from New York. It was the immigrants' children who now began to break out of the big city. Like many young Americans who failed to find jobs near home or who felt they were a burden to their parents, they struck out for the West. As the Jews crossed the continent they learned about an America their parents knew nothing of. Beyond the city ghettos they found that Jews were looked upon as strangers and aliens—and disliked. A New York accent was enough to tag one a "Yid." A degree from City College labeled one both a Jew and a radical. The professions did not welcome Jews, nor did business and industry. Some Jews changed their names or concealed their origin to get work.

The rest of the world, too, was crippled by the Depression. There was mass unemployment throughout Europe. In Poland, the worst-hit were the three million Jews. They suffered additional blows from boycotts and the policies of an anti-Semitic government. A third of Poland's Jews lived below the poverty line, and half of these were starving.

In Germany the world crisis made terrible postwar conditions even worse. The Nazi Party was bidding for leadership on a program that blamed the Jews for all the nation's troubles and promised salvation. By 1933 Adolf Hitler was able to take power and establish a dictatorship.

After thirteen years of furious anti-Semitic propaganda Hitler was ready to carry out his war on the Jews. What he had said he would do, wrote the American Catholic historian Frederick M. Schweitzer, was "only what Christian teaching and preaching had been saying for nearly 2000 years." In power, the Nazis applied a pattern they would use in all other countries they would take over. There were 500,000 Jews in a total German population of 65,000,000. The Nazis expelled Jews from all public places—parks, museums, theaters, concert halls. Social contacts with Gentiles were strictly forbidden. All Jews in public office were dismissed. Jewish businesses were boycotted and so were Jewish doctors, dentist, pharmacists, lawyers, musicians, actors . . . Schools closed their doors to all Jewish children. New racist laws declared Jews could not be considered to be Germans or to have any rights of citizenship. Jews were baited and beaten on the streets, attacked in their homes, tortured, jailed, and murdered. There was no appeal to justice. Hitler was the law.

While there was still time some Jews managed to get out of Germany. Those who fought back were put into concentration camps they never left. Nazi youth goose-stepped to the tune of "Today Germany is ours—tomorrow the world!" Anti-Semitism was Hitler's weapon for world conquest. Nazi agents spread the poison throughout the world. The theme was the "Jewish Bolshevik-capitalist menace." Feverish Jew-baiting abroad followed the brutal example set by the Nazis in Germany. Fascist movements eager for power saw in anti-Semitism the means of achieving it.

The deep wound made by the Depression left Americans more susceptible to the sickness of anti-Semitism. An alarming number of anti-Semitic organizations sprang up, taking strongest hold on the German-Americans and the Irish-Americans. They directed their racist appeal to the unemployed, to the small businessmen and shopkeepers trying to survive against forces they could not understand. Anti-Semitic newspapers, posters, stickers, leaflets flooded the streets and the mails. Many of the fascist groups had ties to the Nazis or were funded by them. They carried such names as the Silver Shirts, the Christian Crusaders, the Christian Front, the Christian Mobilizers, the American Vigilantes, the Black Legion. One of them, the German American Bund, was the American branch of the Nazi Party. Its members wore uniforms and engaged in rifle practice and military drill.

Some of these groups were the creation of local cranks. Others had ties to the Nazis or were funded by them. Still others were financed by industrialists, bankers, and politicians who saw in the Hitler-type propaganda the hope of putting into power a reactionary government, one that would replace the progressive New Deal program of President Roosevelt which they called the "Jew Deal."

Such respected figures as the novelist Theodore Dreiser and the legendary hero-aviator Charles Lindbergh, as well as a number of congressmen, openly voiced anti-Semitism. Jews were attacked as warmongers, Reds, international bankers who controlled America. To investigate the last charge, the business magazine *Fortune* made a survey in 1936 of who owned what in the United States. The results reassured America that its wealth was *not* in Jewish hands.

But facts were of no account to the country's anti-Semites, such as the eloquent Catholic priest Father Charles Coughlin, head of the Christian Front. Every week on his national radio hookup, he hit at a "Jewish conspiracy" to take over America. In his newspaper, *Social Justice*, he repeated the lies Henry Ford had peddled in the twenties.

The Jews became the subject of debate everywhere. Christian opinion on what to do about them or what they should do about themselves ran from one extreme to the other. Some demanded the Jews assimilate to the point where they would disappear as an ethnic group. But others accused Jews of going too far in trying to do exactly that. Still others said there was just no way to solve the "Jewish problem." The best thing the

Jews could do, they advised, would be to leave the United States.

Meanwhile, with the victims of Nazism seeking frantically to escape Hitler's prison house, what did the United States do? From the day Hitler took power till the day America entered World War II about 110,000 refugees were allowed in. Perhaps 100,000 of them were Jewish, less than 2 per cent of the Jewish population here then. It was desperately too few compared with the enormous need. And few as they were, their entrance was opposed by many.

The Jewish agencies helped establish the refugees in their new homeland. Most settled on Manhattan's upper West Side. Later many followed their children to Queens. Unlike the east Europeans, more than half the German Jews were well educated. Among them were scholars, teachers, novelists, artists, dramatists, poets, composers, physicians, scientists. The talented people Hitler expelled from Europe greatly enriched American culture and science.

Why did the United States do so little to rescue Europe's beleaguered Jews in this period? Certainly Roosevelt's New Deal was humanitarian in its policies. The President himself spoke often of his desire to help. But there was a great gap between what he said and what was done. Key members of his administration concerned with policy in this field argued that bringing in many refugees would undermine an already shaky economy. Or it would mean intefering with another country's internal affairs. Or it would interfere with the war effort. Or it would violate the immigration quota system.

Yet the fact was that between 1933 and 1943 there were over 400,000 unfilled places within U.S. immigration quotas for countries under Nazi domination. Each place that went unfilled meant the death of a European Jew. The American tradition of sanctuary for the oppressed was forgotten.

Many Americans in all parts of the country were deeply concerned over Hitler's assault upon the Jews. From 1933 on they bombarded the State Department and the White House with petitions, resolutions, letters, telegrams, condemning Nazi cruelty and urging American action to help the Jews. The response was polite but vague. No action was promised.

The American Jews, of course, tried to save their doomed brothers abroad. They organized rallies across the nation, attacking Nazi racist policies and urging the President to speak a word of warning and condemnation to the German government. The White House remained silent.

Disagreement among the Jews over what to do about the failure to act weakened their pressure upon Roosevelt. He had captured the vote and the loyalty of the liberal Jewish community with his bold program to help the victims of the Depression. Some Jewish leaders called for militant action, for parades, demonstrations, protest rallies. But others opposed such means, preferring to exert influence quietly. Perhaps because they feared to arouse an anti-Semitism just below the surface of popular feeling. The result was they never mustered a powerful enough challenge to force the rescue of more Jews.

The other free nations did not do much better. They too, for whatever reasons, delayed taking action. And millions of those who might have been rescued perished. The will to save stood no chance against Hitler's powerful urge to destroy.

Hatred for the crimes of the Nazis inspired millions in all nations to fight against Hitler. The Jews of America, like their brethren worldwide, had an additional motive. They wanted to avenge the martyrdom of their people. No matter what their age or profession the Jews joined the fight. They took up arms wherever they were, they formed their own brigades, they joined the resistance movements of occupied territories, they worked in the underground. Their uprising in the Warsaw Ghetto in 1943 is one of the great epics of human courage. With no hope of success they held off relentless attack by tanks, infantry, and artillery for thirty-six days. In the end, the ghetto was a dead mass of smoldering ruins.

When the war ended in Germany's defeat, the toll in human life was enormous. All the nations involved suffered

The Jewish people took up arms against fascism
wherever they were. They joined the resistance movements of occupied territories and they worked in the
underground. The uprising in the Warsaw Ghetto in
1943 was one of the great epics of human courage.

terrible losses. But the Jewish people had the highest death rate.

Genocide is not new. There have been massacres almost everywhere in the world and in every century. But nothing was ever so inventively destructive as the holocaust Hitler devised. His complex transportation system, his slave labor program, his extermination camps, the ovens, the Zyklon B method of mass execution—they combined bestiality with the scientific precision of a huge slaughterhouse. The Nazis had set out to exterminate Europe's nine million Jews. They killed six million of them, two out of every three. Put another way, Hitler succeeded in murdering one out of every three of the world's seventeen million Jews. One must stop to think about such huge numbers. Each is a human being, an individual, a life.

Chapter 11

NEXT YEAR IN JERUSALEM

The huge industrial buildup required to meet the military needs of World War II pulled America out of the Depression. Soon after the war ended, working-class standards began to rise and the middle class expanded astonishingly. The postwar refugee-aid program added another 100,000 immigrants to the Jewish population. But after 1948, most Jews desiring to quit Europe, North Africa, or the Near East went not to the United States but to the new state of Israel.

Within the United States, the old ghettos faded fast. As the immigrants climbed from one rung of the economic ladder to the next, they moved to better housing. Exodus from the urban centers to new neighborhoods and to the suburbs accelerated. A great many Jews had become firmly fixed in the middle class. The man once a junk dealer now made auto parts. The small contractor, aided by government-backed loans, became the builder of big housing developments. The petty retailer became the supermarket operator.

The GI Bill of Rights and the expanding economy made it possible for an extremely high percentage of Jewish youth to attend college and go on to graduate school. The university-trained children of immigrants became scientists and engineers, founders of electronic concerns, or members of research teams serving industry or government. Jews entered book and magazine publishing, television and films, advertising and public relations.

As discrimination lessened, Jews moved into professions that

had never accepted them before. They became professors of
literature, historians, physicists, biochemists, sociologists. Their
incomes rose, their living conditions improved, their travels
broadened. When the third generation came of age, it was
clear they were not as interested in the world of private enter-
prise as their parents and grandparents had been. Now they
favored the arts, sciences, and professions—or a role in government—rather than the family business.

What Hitler had done had a profound effect upon the way
Jews thought about themselves. Nazi racism lumped all Jews
together. There was no escape from Jewishness; Hitler had
seen to that. No matter where a man came from, what tongue
he spoke, how many of his ancestors had been Jewish, what
religion or none he might practice. These were only superficial
differences in Hitler's eyes. Jews were one solid international
racial conspiracy to him. And their role as he saw it was to
exploit the Aryan race.

In another sense, Hitler made being Jewish an affirmation
of or identification with everything opposed to Nazism—that
is, everything decent and humane.

What is a Jew, then? In Jewish law it means being born of
Jewish parentage, more particularly, of a Jewish mother, and
being a member of an ethnic group and a religious community.

Others would answer, "He who says he is a Jew, is a Jew."
But what people think of themselves is only part of it. Hitler
took unto himself the making of that decision. He said who
was Jewish and who was not.

Jews have considered themselves to be a race, a religious
group, a nation, a people. Scientifically speaking, there is no
Jewish "race." Anthropologists today offer proof that Jews of
one geographical area share physical traits with their immedi-
ate non-Jewish neighbors, but much less so with Jews of a dis-
tant area. There have been those who argued whether a person
could be a Jew and an American (or a Frenchman or an Irishman or a Russian . . .) while others have answered that of
course a Jew could be an American (or something else) because being Jewish was simply to have a certain religious

faith. Yet when Jews converted to Christianity under the pressure of an Inquisition their enemies persecuted them, insisting they were still Jews. So two wills can make a group, as a sociologist has pointed out—"the self-will that creates unity, and the will of others that imposes a unity where hardly any is felt."

What defines a Jew, then? Religion? Origin? Culture? Language? Commitment to a national homeland? Certainly most American Jews emerged from a single culture, the Yiddish-speaking culture of eastern Europe. But something else linking them—and all Jews throughout the world—is the sense of a common fate. It is the knowledge that they are connected by birth and tradition to a single religion. And that the outside world imposes that common fate on Jews. The sharing of that historical memory was agonizingly strengthened by Hitler's holocaust.

The terrifying example of Hitler Germany swung American Jewry to a pro-Zionist view. The longing for Zion, the ancestral homeland, had been central to Jewish thought and feeling ever since the dispersion. The blessing "Next year in Jerusalem" is part of the Jewish ritual. There was always some physical connection between the Jews and their former homeland; the migration of individual Jews to Palestine never stopped.

Zionism as a political movement, however, did not begin until the 1890s. Earlier, in the 1860s, one Jewish thinker suggested the world owed it to the Jews to establish them in the ancient homeland, and another proposed that Jews plant small agricultural settlements in Palestine as a beginning. But there was no mass movement until thirty-six-year-old Theodore Herzl, a journalist and playwright, published his book *The Jewish State,* in 1896.

Herzl came of a fully assimilated Jewish family in Budapest. Working in Vienna, he saw a poisonous hatred for the Jews reviving. In Paris he was shaken to his depths by the sensational Dreyfus affair which he reported. A Jewish artillery captain was falsely branded a traitor to France and sentenced to life imprisonment on Devil's Island. Anti-Semitism became a nationwide issue. The conviction of Dreyfus was used to proclaim Jews traitorous by nature. It was charged they controlled France and would destroy it. (Years later the incriminating evidence was shown to be a forgery and Captain Dreyfus was restored to his place in the Army and promoted.) Then there were the pogroms rapidly multiplying in eastern Europe. Herzl foresaw the time when the very survival of the Jews would be at stake.

Emancipation of the Jews, Herzl believed, had only guaranteed their rights on paper. Physically freed from the ghetto, many Jews still remained in the ghetto in their attitude. He did not think assimilation was the answer. Wherever Jews lived in any number, there always seemed to be a "Jewish problem." The only solution, he concluded, was to create a Jewish state, to give the Jews sovereignty over a piece of their own land, and let them build their own country.

The movement began with Herzl, and the Zionist congresses he organized opened worldwide discussion of the idea of a national homeland. Herzl died only eight years after his book appeared, but other leaders carried on the struggle.

In the beginning, upper-class Jews in western Europe and in the United States were not interested, or were even hostile to Zionism. They believed whatever country they were part of was their Zion. (The Dreyfus case made many think they had been wrong.) The assimilationists said more civil rights would solve whatever problems they had. The Hasidic Jews waited for the Messiah. Radical Jews believed that changing the system from capitalism to socialism would wipe out all problems, including anti-Semitism.

The American Jews who stemmed from eastern Europe knew its history of legal restrictions and physical massacres. They saw that even when governments changed, Jews could still be treated badly. (Poland shifted from the Tsar's empire to an independent republic and then to a Communist state but anti-Semitism stayed through every stage.) Relatively few immigrant Jews returned to such homelands.

The younger, American-born Jews were at first not interested in Zionism. The movement was scarcely felt here. Europe seemed far off and in America what cause was there for alarm? A change occurred on the eve of World War I when Louis Brandeis, one of America's most respected lawyers (later a Supreme Court justice), decided to devote himself to Zionism. He helped make it a political force. In 1912 Hadassah was formed by Zionist women to promote the cause.

Then in 1917 the British issued the Balfour Declaration, favoring "the establishment in Palestine of a national home for the Jewish people." Lord Balfour, like other British leaders, believed not only that this policy would be to Britain's self-interest in the postwar world, but that Christians owed the Jews—exiled, scattered, persecuted—an "immeasurable debt." The Declaration was greeted with jubilation by the Jewish community in Europe and America. Exactly what the vague terms of the Declaration meant or promised was open to many interpretations. But it gave Zionism a great chance to fulfill its hopes.

Now the dream appeared to be an achievable reality. Thousands of American Jews joined the Zionist movement. The settlements begun in Palestine chiefly by Jews from eastern Europe came to draw their primary financial and political support from America. The Zionist movement grew quite complex, with many federations and political parties of varying views. But they put aside their differences when it came to the practical necessities of raising funds for Zionism.

In the 1930s the actions of the Klan, Henry Ford, Father Coughlin, and a host of other anti-Semites, seen against the backdrop of Hitler Germany, left no American Jew untouched. Could fascism happen here too? Were Jews always to be the outsiders, always to be the victims? That fear fired nationalism among Jews, just as it did among other ethnic minorities who sensed their own separateness, their own isolation.

The problem of establishing a Jewish homeland was not a simple one. There were no empty places anywhere in the world. No matter how noble the motives for immigration, settlement by foreigners is resisted. Arabs as well as Jews lived in Palestine. It had been a Turkish territory until the war's end. Now it was under British protection. To whom was the country to belong? A clash between the two national movements was inevitable. It was not a matter of misunderstanding, but of a natural conflict under such circumstances.

Once Hitler was in power, Zionists did not make any compromise on Jewish immigration to Palestine. In 1933 30,000 Jews entered, the next year 42,000, and the next, 61,000. When Hitler's war and the holocaust ended, the remnants of European Jewry knocked frantically on Palestine's door. It was desperately urgent for them to find a place to live. No government in the world had offered to take them in. The hopes for finding common ground between Arab and Jew seemed buried. In the words of the historian of Zionism, Walter Laqueur, this was the essence of the situation as the Jews saw it:

> The question whether the Jewish people had a right to exist did not occur to them. Bitter experience in eastern Europe had taught them that decisive issues in the history of peoples were not resolved according to abstract principles of justice, and that as long as Jews were a minority they would always be persecuted and permanently in danger of destruction. Before 1933 the question had not arisen so acutely. It was generally believed that there was enough room in Palestine for both Jews and Arabs. But as Arab resistance grew stronger, and simultaneously the pressure of immigration increased, conviction grew among the Zionists that if the national aspirations of Arabs and Jews could not be reconciled, their own case was the stronger, if only because European Jewry was in danger of extermination. The Jews had nowhere to go but to Palestine. The Arabs could be absorbed if necessary in the neighboring countries.

Britain had curbed immigration to Palestine in 1939. It proved disastrous to Jewish refugees fleeing across the Mediterranean. Illegal entry of Jews to Palestine began and by 1947, 113,000 had got past the barred gates. Now there was a violent three-cornered struggle for Palestine among Jews, Arabs, and the British.

The crisis went to the United Nations, which agreed on a partition plan for separate Jewish and Arab states in Palestine, with Jerusalem as an international city. American Zionists played a key role in obtaining its adoption, with the Soviet Union voting in support. The Jews accepted the plan, but not the Arabs. The British left, and the independent state of Israel was proclaimed on May 14, 1948. At once seven Arab states invaded Israel. The war ended in a UN-arranged truce, with Israel holding larger territory than the UN Partition Plan had allotted it. Israel kept the extra territory on the ground that it had won it at a great cost in a war forced upon it by aggressor nations.

Now Israel flung wide its doors to immigrants. The ingathering of exiles moved swiftly. With the help of the Joint Distribution Committee, thousands of new settlers came in from all over the world.

The 1967 and 1973 challenges from the Arab world resulted in two wars. Jews of every view found common cause in their response. The wars tapped Jewish feelings even "among people who didn't know they had any," as one observer put it. They felt Israel's survival meant their survival. It was not a question of allegiance. Most American Jews feel they owe allegiance to the United States, whose citizens they are. But they also feel a solidarity with Israel, and therefore give it their support.

Today the world Jewish population is estimated at about 14,000,000. There are about 2,600,000 Jews living in Israel, and about the same number in the Soviet Union. The Jewish population of the United States is around 6,000,000. "Next year in Jerusalem" is no longer only a dream, yet most American Jews choose to remain in the country where they grew up.

What are their concerns? What are their hopes?

Chapter 12

MYTH AND REALITY

Ask an American what he is and it's likely he will answer he's an Italian, a Swede, a Greek, a Jew. He doesn't think first of his citizenship, but of his ethnic ties. True, American society, especially through its schools, worked to strip the immigrants of their "foreignness," their old habits and culture. The ethnic pattern that separated them was modified, but not wiped out. They still were—and are, down to the third generation and beyond—distinct and identifiable as members of their own ethnic groups. No group has ever been able entirely to discard its past.

The notion of an American melting pot did not work out. The ethnic groups kept some sense of themselves and their unique character even as they were reshaped by new experiences in America. The Jews' past links them to other people of their group. And so do ties created by the special economic, social, and political concerns of their group life in America. Underneath all this, of course, are the emotional bonds of family and of all those who are like oneself—the larger family, the whole ethnic group. To use the Yiddish word, the mishpocheh, the family of blood, of faith, of memory.

Why should all the people who immigrated be fused into one homogeneous mass? Was it really possible? Was it even desirable? Thinkers like Horace Kallen, a Jewish philosopher, pointed out back in 1915 that American society was made up of a variety of cultures. He insisted the immigrant groups had not lost their identity. And that was good, he said, because as each developed its own ethnic life it contributed those special qualities to the larger pattern of American life.

This point of view, called cultural pluralism, gradually won wide support against the melting-pot theory. As Dr. Kallen said, "Since people have to live together, plurality is a basic condition of existence. The need is to bring differences together to make a union, not unity." All voices should not be expected to sing in unison the old Anglo-Saxon theme of "America." What is much better is the orchestration of the many rich and different voices that express the life of each ethnic group.

While American Jews for the most part tried to integrate themselves with American society, certain pressures made them feel their minority position intensely. The effects of prejudice and discrimination, whether active at the moment or not, are imprinted on every Jew. He realizes the outer world does not accept him as an individual. It insists upon fixing the label "Jew" upon him. Regarded as an outsider, he tends to cherish his differences. He feels loyal to his people's historic character and to the source of their being, and sensitive to any threat to his people's survival.

That question of Jewish cultural survival troubles the leaders of the major Jewish organizations. They view assimilation and intermarriage (increasing steadily in recent years) as "grave perils." While there are more Jews in the United States today than ever before, the birth rate among Jews is lower than for other ethnic groups. The proportion of Jews to the general American population was at its height in 1937 (3.7 per cent) and has been shrinking ever since (2.9 per cent in 1967). The rise in divorce rates is also seen to weaken the Jewish family. Most families, regardless of religion, suffer damage through divorce. But Jews feel more threatened because they believe the close-knit family unit is what preserved them while other peoples perished.

One remedy offered is a more intensive Jewish education, in the home and in the school. More than half a million Jews are enrolled in some form of Jewish education. All-day Jewish schools, which include a secular curriculum, are spreading again. The number of Jewish studies programs offered at high schools and colleges is rapidly rising. Acting on their own, students at scores of colleges have established "free Jewish universities" outside official jurisdiction. Partly as a result, more than three hundred colleges now offer such credit courses. Many present contemporary issues as well as the traditional Jewish history, philosophy, and Hebrew language courses. The 400,000 Jewish college students are now offered Jewish religious, cultural, and counseling programs on hundreds of campuses. There is an awakened interest too in the Yiddish language, which is being taught at several colleges. Not counting seminary faculties, there are perhaps 250 major academic posts in the new field of Jewish studies, for which there are numerous doctoral programs.

How Jews are portrayed in the historical education of Americans is of great importance. The Jews have been ignored or misrepresented in the school and college texts. Most Americans know nothing about the evolution of Judaism and Jewish culture, and of the mistreatment of the Jews by the majority through the ages. The textbook publishers are way behind in giving Jews their historical due.

A special aspect of this problem was the treatment of Jews in Catholic teaching materials. In 1965 the Ecumenical Council Vatican II issued a historical declaration on the Church's attitude toward Jews. It absolved the Jewish people from the charge of deicide—collective guilt in the death of Jesus—that has historically been a major cause of anti-Semitism. Catholic textbooks since that time have been portraying Jews in a positive light, and telling the students what Christians did to Jews during the Crusades and the Spanish Inquisition. There is still scanty material, however, on the Nazi holocaust and the founding of the state of Israel.

The relations between blacks and Jews—America's two most prominent ethnic minorities—have been a matter of great concern in recent years. Both minorities have tried to gain equality in an America hostile to racial and cultural differences. Jews have been victimized by a Christian world and blacks by a

white world. But in America their history has followed very
different courses. Blacks came in chains, and Jews as free
people. The small number of Jews suffered relatively few dis-
abilities in early America, while the millions of blacks were
enslaved for 150 years. For the brief decade of Reconstruction,
blacks tasted freedom and equality. Then the nation stripped
them of their rights and ghettoized them.

It was just at that time that the mass immigration of Jews
to America began. The newcomers assumed that by hard work
they could realize the American dream of success. And as white
Americans they did, for the most part, come to enjoy the rights
and privileges a white skin brings—the rights and privileges
denied anybody who is black.

It was not until the mass migration of southern blacks to the
North during World War I that Jews and blacks came into
close contact in the cities. As the Jews moved up the economic
ladder, the blacks remained below. The difference in their
fortunes became far more striking than the common factor of
oppression in their histories. It could not help but affect the
encounter between black American and Jewish American.

That many Jews "made it" in America while most blacks did
not was not the fault of the blacks. It was the crime of white
racism, a racism that many Jews, as white Americans, share.
Among the white groups, however, the Jewish record of participation in the struggle for black equality has been outstanding.
The part Jews played in the civil rights movement of the sixties
was far out of proportion to their numbers.

In the relation between individual Jews and blacks, the
blacks have usually been at a disadvantage: landlord-tenant,
merchant-consumer, housewife-domestic, teacher-student, social worker-client. Recently, in many of the jobs and neighborhoods blacks aspire to, they find Jews there before them. From
the friction engendered by these situations comes feelings of
hostility, of anti-Jewishness. It is easy to forget that it is the
employer as employer, the landlord as landlord, the merchant
as merchant who is exploiting one in that capacity, and not *as*
a Jew. And it is equally easy to forget that where employer,

Jewish Americans have maintained their cultural identity, which has played an important part in their survival.

landlord, and merchant are *not* Jewish, the exploitation of the black is no less evident.

That Jews (and other white ethnic groups) have been discriminated against, no one can deny. But such experiences cannot be equated with the injustices suffered by black Americans. The facts are too plain: Jews have a higher percentage of college and graduate students than the general population. They are more heavily concentrated in white-collar occupations and the professions. They have a higher family income.

Jews achieved this status in large part by the sacrifices made by the immigrant generation eager to shape a better life for their children and grandchildren. By self-help and community help they made their way up. But even though handicapped as an ethnic minority, they benefited by being part of the privileged white majority. They made their way on merit, in competition with other whites. But eliminated from that competition were blacks.

Today blacks challenge white privilege. They demand the equality denied them for centuries. They are not seeking special privilege; they are simply trying to overcome the intolerable results of the special privilege accorded whites all this time. That is why affirmative action is needed to increase their educational and employment opportunities.

When goals are proposed for affirmative action, they rouse fear among Jews because they sound like quotas. And Jews have had bitter experience with quotas. They cannot forget the quota system in Russia and Poland, or in the universities and medical schools of America, which shut them out. Quotas by any name are bad. To impose new injustices as a remedy for old ones only creates new and worse problems.

It will be unfortunate if Jews and blacks compete with each other for a larger share of a shrinking pie. Better for each, and for the country too, would be a united struggle of all minorities to enlarge the pie. What is needed is to expand the economy, to reorder national priorities, to provide more jobs, more housing, better schools.

All the talk of "making it" obscures the fact that many immigrants did not attain the success the popular myth would have us believe. The Jews became the example of how open the American system was to disadvantaged groups. But the fact is that even now there is considerable poverty among American Jews. Studies made in the early seventies revealed that in New York City there were about 250,000 Jews below the poverty level of $3500, and another 150,000 more who earned less than $4500. About half of them were aged. They made up the third largest group of poor people in the city, after the blacks and the Puerto Ricans. Estimates of the number of Jews in the U.S.A. living in poverty ranged up to one million. The newspapers spoke of them as "the forgotten poor," and an official of the American Jewish Congress admitted that "we in the Jewish community also labored under the myth of universal Jewish affluence." Jews in the large cities began to call for channeling public and Jewish social agency funds into food and health programs, community centers, and housing projects to serve the Jews without money.

In the end, then, what general statement can be made about American Jews? There is no one we can point to as the typical Jew. For American Jews are a mixture of Jews from many different cultural backgrounds and places in the world. What the American experience has made of them varies from person to person. And as that experience is always changing, so too are its effects.

That Jews are prominent in so many fields far out of proportion to their numbers is one fact the world is familiar with. One reason is the traditional devotion of Jews to education. But more important is their liberation from restrictions that crippled them for so many generations. Emancipation freed their creative powers. Their pent-up energy exploded. From their ranks came one after another to achieve eminence in the labor and liberal movements, in business and finance, in literature and music, in art and architecture, in law and medicine, in science and technology, in scholarship and publishing, in politics and philosophy.

What the future may hold for American Jews was put well

by Rabbi Robert Gordis: "Any society that sustains variety and encourages innovation, for whatever reason, will offer a favorable climate for Jews, while any society that is inhospitable to variety and fearful of change will be hostile to Jews and their presence in its midst."